P-40 Warhawk Aces of the CBI

SERIES EDITOR: TONY HOLMES

OSPREY AIRCRAFT OF THE ACES • 35

P-40 Warhawk Aces of the CBI

Carl Molesworth

OSPREY
AVIATION

Front Cover
At 1444 hours on 24 April 1943, the Japanese 1st Air Brigade, located at bases in the Hankow area, launched 44 Ki-43 'Oscars' of the 25th and 33rd Sentais on a raid against the USAAF base at Ling Ling. The weather had been bad all month, with low cloud and heavy rain, but on this Saturday before Easter the conditions improved just enough for the Japanese to mount their attack. The 'Oscar' fighters made the 200-mile run south-west to Ling Ling, with plans to pass east of the base and then turn back toward the north-west so as to carry out a surprise attack from an unlikely direction. By employing such a ruse, the Japanese hoped to catch most American aircraft still on the ground. Unfortunately for the Ki-43 pilots, the local Chinese air warning network had tracked their progress all the way from Hankow, giving the 23rd Fighter Group's 75th Fighter Squadron plenty of time to launch 14 P-40Ks in defence of its base at Ling Ling.

The American pilots intercepted the attackers some ten miles south-east of their airfield, and according to the 75th's squadron history, the 'Oscars' went into a formation that the P-40 pilots called the 'squirrel cage' (similar to a Lufbery circle). Whenever an American pilot attempted to take a shot at a Ki-43 there would be several more ready to swing in behind him. The Japanese pilots showed unusually good discipline, making it difficult for the P-40 pilots to stay in a firing position long enough to get off a telling burst. Nevertheless, ranking 75th FS ace Capt John Hampshire succeeded in claiming one 'Oscar' destroyed, as did three other pilots from the squadron. No P-40s were lost in return, despite the Japanese claiming three destroyed.

The fight lasted an extraordinarily long 55 minutes, and towards the end of it a twin-engined 'fighter' (most likely a Ki-46 'Dinah' of the 18th Independent Air Squadron) flew over Ling Ling dropping propaganda leaflets which challenged the P-40 pilots to a 'decisive air battle'! This aircraft was subsequently shot down by John Hampshire after he had chased it for over 100 miles
(*cover artwork by Iain Wyllie*)

First published in Great Britain in 2000 by Osprey Publishing, Elms Court, Chapel Way Botley, Oxford, OX2 9LP
E-mail: info@ospreypublishing.com

ISBN 1 84176 079 X

Edited by Tony Holmes
Page design by TT Designs, T & B Truscott
Cover Artwork by Iain Wyllie
Aircraft Profiles by James Laurier
Scale Drawings by Mark Styling
Origination by Grasmere Digital Imaging, Leeds, UK
Printed through Bookbuilders, Hong Kong

00 01 02 03 04   10 9 8 7 6 5 4 3 2 1

ACKNOWLEDGEMENTS
The author offers his sincere thanks to the many veterans of service in the China-Burma-India Theatre who provided the photographs, documents and personal recollections that made this book possible. They are;

23rd FG – George Barnes, Sully Barrett, Jack Best, Hollis Blackstone, Dallas Clinger, Art Cruikshank, Henry Davis, Victor Gelhausen, Joe Griffin, Bill Grosvenor, Bill Harris, Bill Hawkins, Tex Hill, Don Hyatt, Bruce Holloway, Bill Johnson, Luther Kissick, Leon Klesman, Jim Lee, Marvin Lubner, Don Lopez, Ward McMillen, Forrest Parham, Don Quigley, Ed Rector, Elmer Richardson, John Rosenbaum, G H Steidle, John Stewart, Dick Templeton, Don Van Cleve, Art Waite, John Wheeler and J M Williams.

51st FG – Fred Altiere, Dale Bleike, Lyle Boley, Roy Brown, Fred Burgett, Bob Conden, Harvey Elling, Bill Evans, Tom Glasgow, Clair Goddard, Jack Hamilton, Hazen Helvey, Francis Hirchert, Ken Hoylman, K C Hynds, Bob Liles, Lynn Marshall, Jack Muller, Ed Nollmeyer, Bill Norberg, Paul Royer, Roy Santin, Gordon Spence, Charles Streit, Stan Strout, Jim Thorn, Charlie Urquhart, Paul Wedlan and Charles White.

80th FG – Phil Adair, Hal Doughty, Bob Gale, Bill Harrell, Pat Randall, Harland Running, Dodd Shepard and Ralph Ward.

CACW – Bill Bonneaux, Glenn Burnham, Ray Callaway, Bill Colman, Dick Daggett, Gene Girton, John Hamre, Jim Kidd, Armit Lewis, S Y Liu, Charles Lovett, Bill Mustill, Homer Nunley, E J Phillips, Santo Savoca, Wildy Stiles and Charles Wright.

Others who contributed material include Jack Cook, Jane Dahlberg, D J Klaasen, Steve Moseley, Ed Reed and Dwayne Tabatt.

I also would like to recognise the work of authors John M Andrade, Martha Byrd, Wanda Cornelius, Daniel Ford, F F Liu, Steve Muth, Frank Olynyk, Malcolm Rosholt, Kenn C Rust, Duane Schultz and Thayne Short. Finally, the Air Force Historical Research Agency and Maxwell Air Force Base provided invaluable historical records compiled by the units involved.

CONTENTS

For a catalogue of all titles published by Osprey Publishing please contact us at:

Osprey Direct UK, P.O. Box 140, Wellingborough, Northants NN8 4ZA, UK • E-mail: info@ospreydirect.co.uk

Osprey Direct USA, P.O. Box 130, Sterling Heights, MI 48311-0130, USA • E-mail: info@ospreydirectusa.com

Or visit our website: **www.ospreypublishing.com**

INTRODUCTION

Military historians have not always been kind to the Curtiss P-40, the US Army Air Force's frontline fighter at the start of America's involvement in World War 2. The P-40 was caught on the ground at Pearl Harbor and was badly mauled by Japanese A6M Zero fighters over the Philippines and Java. In the year that followed, P-40 pilots barely managed to hold the line in northern Australia and New Guinea until new fighters with higher performance became available.

Yet in one remote corner of the war the P-40 Warhawk compiled a combat record as good as the finest fighter types of its era. In so doing, it captured the imagination and adoration of the American public as few warplanes ever have. These P-40s were, of course, the ones flown in the China-Burma-India Theatre. Operated first by Claire Lee Chennault's legendary American Volunteer Group (AVG), and later by American and Chinese pilots of the Tenth and Fourteenth Air Forces, the P-40 simply dominated the skies over Burma and China. They were able to establish air superiority over free China, northern Burma and the Assam Valley of India in 1942, and they never relinquished it.

This book will not cover the AVG in detail, for that is a subject worthy of its own volume in this series. If, however, one includes the AVG's score in a tally of confirmed aerial victories in the CBI, P-40 pilots were credited with 973 kills – 64.8 per cent of all the enemy aeroplanes shot down by American pilots in this theatre.

Numbers such as these are important in any discussion of fighter aircraft and pilots. Strategies, tactics, conditions and personalities all have their place as well. But in the final analysis, it always boils down to the same question for a fighter pilot returning from a mission – 'How many did you get?'

Unfortunately, answering that question accurately wasn't always easy for a tired pilot just back from the swirling confusion of an air battle. What he thought he saw and what he remembered might not even agree with an account of the same engagement given by his wingman. It was left to the squadron intelligence officers to gather the stories and try to sort them out. The Tenth and Fourteenth Air Forces adhered to the same standards for confirming aerial victories as were used in other theatres of war, but the confirmation process was an inexact science at best.

Knowing that, the historian must view the numbers of confirmations credited to individual pilots, and their units, with caution. Those numbers give us a relative scale by which to judge performance, but that's about as far as they go. For instance, a list in the appendices of this book shows that three pilots tied as the top-scoring P-40 aces in the CBI with 13 confirmed victories apiece. In truth, it is impossible to establish that each of those men shot down precisely 13 aeroplanes, but there is no doubt in the author's mind that all three were superlative fighter pilots.

Likewise, the title 'ace' requires careful handling. In the USAAF, it was conferred unofficially on pilots with five confirmed aerial victories. The number is arbitrary, yet it bears up very well statistically as a measure of achievement in air-to-air combat. On the other hand, ace status cannot be taken as the full measure of an American fighter pilot in the CBI, because a large percentage of them had little or no opportunity to engage enemy aircraft in the sky. The CBI was primarily a fighter-bomber show. Even the most successful aces in the theatre spent more time bombing and strafing ground targets than in air-to-air combat.

Fortunately for the fighter pilots of the Tenth and Fourteenth Air Forces, some of the same traits that hampered the P-40's performance in air-to-air combat made it an excellent ground-attack aircraft. Even the fighter's detractors acknowledge that it was fast at low altitudes, heavily armed and extremely tough. More importantly, the Curtiss P-40 was available in quantity at a time when other American fighters were not. Whether the pilots liked the P-40 or not, it was the aeroplane they had to fly, and they flew it gloriously.

Carl Molesworth
Washington
August 2000

CHINA AIR TASK FORCE

The Curtiss P-40 Warhawk, with a fearsome sharksmouth painted on its distinctive engine cowling, is one of the enduring images of World War 2. It was a handsome bird, with its pointed snout, tapered wings and voluptuously rounded tail surfaces. In photographs, paintings and even cartoons, the P-40 came to symbolise America's war effort – tough, cocky and colourful.

Ironically, the P-40 design had its roots in the earlier blunt-nosed Curtiss Model 75 Hawk fighter, which was powered by a radial engine. The Model H-75 was designed in 1934-35 and entered service with the US Army Air Corps (USAAC) in 1938 as the P-36. It was an excellent peacetime fighter, with pleasant handling characteristics and a top speed of just over 300 mph. In addition, its air-cooled engine made it a relatively simple aircraft to maintain. By 1939, however, the approach of war in Europe had led Great Britain and Germany to introduce fighter designs with performance far beyond the P-36's capabilities. The British Spitfire and German Bf 109, in particular, were sleek machines, powered by liquid-cooled inline engines.

The USAAC, recognising the need to upgrade and expand its fighter forces, issued a request for proposals from the American aircraft industry for a new type that would be on a par with contemporary European designs. Curtiss proposed replacing the P-36's radial engine with the new Allison V-1710 liquid-cooled powerplant. The Army liked the idea – especially the fact that Curtiss could produce the new fighter quickly – and issued a contract for more than 500 aircraft. Thus, the P-40 was born.

Although the inline-engine boosted the Curtiss fighter's top speed by nearly 50 mph, trade-offs were made in other areas of its performance when compared with the P-36. Its greater weight slowed the rate of climb and reduced manoeuvrability, but worst of all, the Allison engine produced its optimum performance at just 15,000 ft – far below the operational ceilings of contemporary European and Japanese fighters. This wasn't the fault of the engine so much as it was the product of outdated thinking on the part of the USAAC, which still saw fighters as medium-altitude, short-ranged weapons of war.

Despite its shortcomings, the first P-40s began to arrive at Army fighter bases in May 1940. Pilots initially found the type both tricky to take-off and land until they became accustomed to the high torque of its engine and the narrow track of its landing gear. However, whilst in the air they were most impressed by the high speeds the P-40 attained in the dive.

Just as Curtiss began gearing up for production of the new fighter, World War 2 erupted in Europe. With America's future allies struggling to defend themselves against the onslaught of Germany's *Blitzkrieg*, Great Britain, France, Greece and several other countries looked to the

United States for help, and the nation's industries responded. Curtiss signed contracts to manufacture an export version of the P-40, which the company called the Model H-81 and the Royal Air Force named the Tomahawk. Most of the latter aircraft would be sent to fight in North Africa, although 100 examples were duly reassigned to China, where they would equip the American Volunteer Group (AVG) in 1941-42.

In 1940, Curtiss redesigned its P-40 to take advantage of a more pow-erful new version of the Allison engine, the V-1710-39. The fighter (des-ignated H-87) boasted a new fuselage design, with a lower thrust line and a bigger cockpit, and all of its guns were mounted in the wings. The British called the new design the Kittyhawk, and in American service it was known informally as the Warhawk. All future P-40 models – and they would be numerous – were modifications of the original H-87 design.

The P-40 was never the best performing fighter in the sky, but it was reliable, carried heavy armament, and could withstand amazing amounts of battle damage and still bring its pilot home safely. By the time produc-tion ended in 1944, Curtiss had built more than 15,000 P-40s of all types, which had duly flown with more Allied nations than any other combat aircraft of World War 2.

Some pilots loved the P-40 for what it was and others hated it for what it wasn't, but no one could ignore the outstanding combat record com-piled by Warhawk pilots worldwide. They simply flew the fighter that was made available to them, and they fought well with it. Nowhere was this truer than in the dangerous skies of the China-Burma-India Theatre.

CHINA'S LONG WAR

The Japanese had already been fighting in Asia for more than a decade when the surprise attack on Pearl Harbor on 7 December 1941 drew the United States into World War 2. Japan's aggression began in September 1931 with the island nation's capture of Mukden in north-east China. By early 1932 the entire province of Manchuria (China's mineral and indus-trial heart) was under Japanese control. Infrequent clashes occurred between Japanese and Chinese troops throughout the mid-1930s, despite treaty terms limiting Japan to the areas north of the Great Wall. Then in 1937 open warfare between Japan and China resumed.

Fearing that rival nationalist and communist forces in China were about to merge, which would render the nation too strong to subdue by force, the Japanese Army incited an exchange of gunfire with Chinese troops at the Marco Polo Bridge, near Peking, on 7 July 1937. Within a matter of days Japanese ground forces began pouring into China, and a full-scale war was underway. The fighting went badly for the Chinese forces under Generalissimo Chiang Kai-shek. Peking quickly fell, fol-lowed by Nanking in December 1937, then the major port of Canton and the inland city of Hankow in October 1938. Hainan Island, in the South China Sea, was invaded in February 1939, by which time most active resistance on the Chinese mainland had ceased. Japan then turned its attention back to Manchuria, where it fought a bitter engagement against the Soviet Union from May through to September 1939.

Chiang retreated deep into western China, setting up his capital at Chungking, in Szechuan Province, and millions of Chinese refugees fol-lowed him there. Japan now occupied all major Chinese seaports, plus

Claire Lee Chennault looked every bit the legendary figure he was. Seen here in a 1944 photograph, he rose from obscurity to worldwide fame in 1941-42 as commander of the American Volunteer Group, and went on to command the USAAF's China Air Task Force and Fourteenth Air Force

transportation hubs throughout eastern China. Chiang was cut off from the outside world, except for a thin supply line that ran overland for 800 miles from the British-controlled Burmese port of Rangoon through to Kunming, in south-west China. This route would soon become known to the world as 'The Burma Road'.

The Chinese Air Force (CAF) had made a respectable showing for itself during the fighting against Japan, flying aircraft imported from the United States, the Soviet Union, Italy and elsewhere. A key element in its sporadic success was the influence of retired USAAC pilot, Capt Claire Lee Chennault, who came to China in 1937 to serve as Director of Combat Training for the CAF. Chennault set up flying schools, advised Chiang on aircraft purchases and devised an air-raid warning system. According to some sources, Chennault also flew reconnaissance missions, and may have even engaged the Japanese in aerial combat, although his combat record has never been confirmed.

China's small air force was eventually overwhelmed by the increasing numbers of modern combat aircraft that Japan committed to win the war. A series of air raids against Chungking began in April 1940, and soon a new Japanese Navy fighter type in the form of the Mitsubishi A6M Zero-sen mopped up what was left of the CAF's air defences. By that time, however, Chennault had gained a wealth of knowledge about the capabilities of Japanese aircraft, as well as the strategies and tactics employed by Japanese airmen and their leaders.

Stirred by the wanton destruction that the Chinese had suffered at the hands of the Japanese, Chennault was determined to put this information to good use. In October 1940 he travelled to Washington, DC to work with Chinese ambassador T V Soong on selling the United States on a new plan for bolstering China's air defences.

AMERICAN VOLUNTEER GROUP

The plan was simple. With modern American fighters, and pilots to fly them and technicians to keep them in the air, Chiang would have an instant air force. However, with the war in Europe not going well for the Allies, there were no aircraft available for an 'obscure' conflict in Asia.

Technically, the United States still remained neutral, but its factories were turning out desperately needed war materials day and night for export to the British, and for America's own military build-up. Added to these factors was another hurdle facing Chennault and Soong – relations between the United States and Japan were fraying, and politicians in Washington were loath to take any action that might make matters worse. Nevertheless, by the end of the year Chennault and Soong had prevailed.

The deal between the United States and China did not give Chiang Kai-shek everything he wanted, but it did give him what he needed most – 100 fighter aircraft to defend the Burma Road from Japanese air attacks, thus keeping the battered nation's last supply line open. Volunteer American military pilots and groundcrewmen would be allowed to resign from their services and sign a one-year contract to fly for China. Their aircraft would be Tomahawks, an export version of the Curtiss P-40 that equipped many US Army fighter units. Chennault would serve as commanding officer of the unit, which was to be called the American Volunteer Group (AVG).

AVG recruiters quickly fanned out to Army, Navy and Marine airfields throughout the United States and began to sign up volunteers. Meanwhile, arrangements were made to ship the crated Tomahawks by sea to Rangoon, in Burma, where they would be assembled. In July 1941, AVG pilots and groundcrews began training at a remote Burmese jungle base built by the RAF at Toungoo, 200 miles up the Sittang River from Rangoon. By the time Japan attacked Pearl Harbor in early December, the AVG was well versed in Chennault's tactics for fighting the enemy.

Immediately following the attack Chennault split his force to provide protection for both ends of the Burma Road. He placed one squadron in Rangoon to fly alongside the RAF units based at the great port city, and moved the two remaining AVG squadrons to Kunming, which was in range of Japanese air units based in northern French Indo-China.

Two weeks later, the AVG fought its first engagement when a small force of unescorted Ki-48 'Lily' twin-engined bombers attacked Kunming on the morning of 20 December 1941. AVG Tomahawks caught the bombers as they were withdrawing from their target, and a frenzied attack took place. When it ended, the AVG pilots were credited with four confirmed victories and two probable victories for no losses.

The American press, starved of news about US military success in the opening weeks of the war, described the Kunming interception as a great victory. Within days of the engagement *Time* magazine dubbed the AVG 'The Flying Tigers', and so the legend was born. When photos of the AVG's sharkmouthed Tomahawks started appearing in the press, the American public's interest and affection grew.

Japanese attention now shifted to the other end of the Burma Road. Flying from newly-captured airfields in Thailand, and boasting a significant fighter presence, bombers attacked Rangoon on 23 and 25 December. The AVG's 3rd Pursuit Squadron (PS), along with the RAF's Brewster Buffalo-equipped No 67 Sqn, successfully intercepted both raids. Indeed, pilots from the 3rd PS alone claimed no fewer than 35 victories in total, further embellishing the AVG's growing reputation.

The AVG continued to fight over Rangoon for two months, but despite its successes in the air, British and colonial ground forces were unable to halt the Japanese advance into Burma. Rangoon fell on 9 March 1942, and the AVG began fighting a rear-guard withdrawal northward towards China. One by one, the airbases at Toungoo, Magwe, Prome and Lashio were captured, and with the evacuation of Loiwing on 1 May, the AVG lost its last airfield west of the Salween River. From then until it disbanded two months later, the AVG operated from China proper.

ENTER THE USAAF

The weather had been nasty in the Hsiang River Valley for much of the time since the AVG had fled Burma. Even this far north, in China's Hunan Province, thick clouds and rain marked the arrival of the monsoon season. In spite of the weather, the AVG's 2nd PS at Hengyang airfield had managed to launch a successful mission on the morning of 22 June, pilots strafing vessels hauling Japanese cargo north up the Yangtze River. By this late stage in the AVG's brief history, the 2nd PS had re-equipped with the P-40E Warhawk, which was considered superior to the original AVG Tomahawk in the ground-attack role because of its heavier armament of six 0.50-cal machine guns and ability to carry bombs on external racks under the wings and fuselage.

The Warhawks, led by Vice Sqn Ldr Ed Rector, returned to Hengyang late in the morning, and they were still in the process of being refuelled and re-armed at 1320 hrs when the Chinese warning net reported a force of 14 Ki-27 'Nates' (known to the Japanese Army Air Force as the Type 97 fighter) bearing down on the airfield. Rector frantically called the 1st PS (based at Kweilin, 50 miles farther west along the river) for help, then pulled together a flight of seven Warhawks to intercept the incoming enemy force. The pilots scrambled were Rector and three members of his squadron – Charlie Sawyer of the 1st PS, Robert 'Catfish' Raines of the 3rd PS, and newcomer Capt Albert J 'Ajax' Baumler of the USAAF.

At the time of the Pearl Harbor attack, the only American air units east of the International Dateline were stationed in the Philippine Islands. It did not escape notice in Washington that although the P-40s of the Army's 24th Pursuit Group were quickly pummelled by the Japanese over the Philippines, Chennault's AVG was having great success with the same aircraft type over Burma and China. It was also well known in Washington that the AVG was not a permanent unit. When the group's personnel contracts expired in early July 1942, the unit would disband and the Army would assume responsibility for the air war in China. Looking ahead, the Army sent a handful of its pilots to China to fly with the AVG and learn what they could.

'Ajax' Baumler was one of them, although he differed from the other pilots sent to the AVG in that he had already seen combat. Initially serving with the USAAC in the mid-1930s, he resigned his commission to fly fighters with the Republicans in Spain in 1936-37. Scoring 4.5 kills during his seven months in the frontline, Baumler then returned to the USA and rejoined the USAAC. He again resigned his commission in 1941 in order to join the AVG, but his first attempt to reach China was thwarted by the Pearl Harbor attack, and he rejoined the Army instead. However, he soon wangled an assignment to China as a member of an as-yet 'paper' organisation – the 23rd Pursuit Group. Baumler finally arrived in Kunming in May 1942, and by the following month he had made his way to the AVG's easternmost base, Hengyang.

As AVG engagements go, the air battle near Hengyang on 22 June 1942 was successful, but not extraordinary. Bad weather prevented the P-40s at Kweilin from reaching Hengyang to join the fight, so Rector and his men had to go it alone. A definitive record of the fight has not survived, but four Japanese fighters were claimed destroyed for no losses. The citation for 'Ajax' Baumler's first Air Medal credits him with one Ki-27 destroyed that day, this solitary victory not only making Baumler an ace, but also giving him the distinction of being the first USAAF pilot to being credited with a confirmed kill in the China-Burma-India Theatre. One of the early stalwarts of the aerial campaign in the CBI, Baumler would create an impressive record as both a fighter pilot and squadron commander in China during the tumultuous year ahead.

GOODBYE TO THE AVG

On 4 July 1942 (less than two weeks after Baumler's victory) the AVG ceased to exist. The following months would prove to be a testing time for the Allies in China, for the USAAF unit created to replace the AVG – the 23rd FG – was still understrength and lacking in combat experience. Senior officers within the Tenth Air Force, headquartered in India, had failed in their attempts to recruit the AVG en masse following the army air force's arrival in theatre. Indeed, only Chennault himself, five pilots, and a handful of ground personnel agreed to stay on in China as members of the USAAF.

Now world-famous because of the success of the AVG, Chennault was named commanding officer of the Tenth Air Force's China Air Task Force (CATF), and given the rank of brigadier general. He was 49 years old, in only fair health, and nearly exhausted after five years of fighting the Japanese. The CATF was a tiny force, consisting of the P-40-equipped 23rd FG and the 11th Bomb Squadron (Medium) with B-25s. The 23rd FG's initial complement of aircraft comprised a mixed batch of 48 H-81 Tomahawks and P-40Es left behind by the AVG – these would equip the 74th, 75th and 76th FSs. Within a few days of the CATF's formation, the 16th FS of the India-based 51st FG (see Chapter 2) arrived in China with 16 P-40E-1s to serve on detached duty with the 23rd FG.

Boasting a force of just 70 aircraft, the CATF faced a formidable enemy. The Japanese flanked Chiang Kai-shek's free China to the east, south and west, whilst to the north was the Soviet Union, which maintained neutrality with Japan. The loss of Burma in the spring had severed China's last supply link to the outside world, so nothing could move in or out of the country by road, rail or ship. The only avenue left was the air.

Following the fall of Rangoon, transport aircraft began plying the hazardous 450-mile route from Chabua, in India's remote Assam Valley, over the rugged Himalayan Mountains to Kunming. They brought in everything from ammunition and gasoline to toothpaste and toilet paper for the fighting forces in China via this route, which soon became known worldwide as 'The Hump'. It was vital to keep this last supply line open, so the CATF's top priority was to protect the Hump's transport aircraft, and its eastern terminus at Kunming, from enemy air attacks. In addition, the CATF was expected to provide air support for Chinese ground forces facing the Japanese along the border with Burma and in central China.

Although Chennault's force was small and his supplies meagre, he did have a couple of elements working in his favour. A key part of his grand plan was the maintenance of an air-raid warning net throughout his area of operations. The net was a complex web of ground observers, many of them Chinese civilians, arranged in a grid pattern and linked by telephone and radio. Chennault had begun setting up the warning net soon after arriving in theatre in 1937, and as a result, many of the observers in eastern China were now located behind enemy lines. Under the direction of radio expert John Williams, the net was greatly expanded from 1940 onwards, the

When the 23rd FG was activated in July 1942, it adapted the Disney-designed AVG tiger, which was already applied to most of its 'hand-me-down' P-40s, for its own insignia by adding the Uncle Sam top hat, the shredded Japanese flag and the CAF sun. This application, seen on a 74th FS P-40E, was typical of the period

Three of the 74th FS's original pilots were, from left, 2Lts Arthur W Cruikshank Jr and Robert E Turner, and 1Lt Charles L Bair. Cruikshank scored his first victory on 28 December 1942, and went on to become the first ace to score all his kills with the 74th. Turner scored one victory in 1943 flying with the 16th FS, and although Bair led many missions for the squadron, he never registered a claim

information gleaned being fed into command centres, where intercept directors used it to lead Chennault's modest fighter force towards approaching Japanese formations.

It was said that the net worked so well that when Japanese aircraft took off from their bases around Hankow, Chennault would know about it within minutes in Kunming, some 800 miles away. Only on rare occasions did the net fail to give advance warning of enemy air raids. His confidence in the net allowed Chennault to spread his meagre forces to advanced airbases near enemy lines with little fear of having them caught on the ground and destroyed.

The location and quality of Chennault's airfields in China also worked to his advantage. Like the warning net, Chennault's network of airbases was a constant 'work in progress'. Kunming, in Yunnan Province, served not only as the point of entry for Hump flights arriving in China but also as the headquarters for Chennault and the CATF. From Kunming, it was roughly 300 miles south-west to Lashio, the most advanced enemy airbase in Burma, 330 miles south to Hanoi, another enemy stronghold, and 380 miles north to Chungking, Chiang Kai-shek's capital city.

Flying eastward from Kunming to the CATF's other primary bases, it was 425 miles to Kweilin, 105 miles farther to Ling Ling and 65 miles beyond there to Hengyang. From these three bases, the CATF could strike at the Japanese in Canton and Hong Kong on the coast, and up north in the Hankow area. Literally dozens of other airfields were either available for Chennault's immediate use, or were under construction. Several of these were located behind Japanese lines in unoccupied areas controlled by Chinese guerrilla forces.

Virtually all the airfields in China featured crushed gravel runways built by hand. They weren't as smooth as paved surfaces, and they were hard on aircraft tyres, but they were nearly impossible to destroy. A direct hit by a bomb might gouge a hole in the runway, but within minutes a large crew of Chinese workers would descend on the damaged area with picks and shovels, wheelbarrows and hand-drawn rollers. The runway could be back in service by the time the bomber had returned to its base.

Perhaps the most important ace in Chennault's hand at the birth of the CATF was the small contingent of AVG personnel who agreed to join the Army and stay on with him in China. Only five pilots were in this group, but they gave Chennault the core leadership he needed in order to build the new squadrons of the 23rd FG. Majs Frank Schiel Jr, David L 'Tex' Hill and Edward F Rector would command the 74th, 75th and 76th FSs respectively, while Maj John G 'Gil' Bright would assist Hill in the 75th FS and Capt Charles W Sawyer would serve with Rector in the 76th FS. In addition, 18 AVG pilots agreed to delay their departure from China for two weeks following 4 July, providing the CATF with enough flyers to hold the line until additional Army pilots arrived.

Maj Edward F Rector was one of just five AVG pilots to accept Army commissions and stay on in China when the 'Flying Tigers' disbanded. He served as commander of the 76th FS/23rd FG from July through to November 1942, then returned to China in 1944 and commanded the 23rd FG through to the end of the war. Rector claimed 4.75 kills with the AVG and three victories with the 23rd FG

This Hawk 81-A2 (CAF serial P-8194) was the personal mount of leading AVG ace, and 1st PS CO, Sqn Ldr Bob Neale. 'Old No 7' was passed onto the 75th FS following the AVG's disbandment on 4 July 1942, and Neale continued to fly it for a further two weeks before finally leaving China. The 13-victory ace claimed one kill and four probables with this aircraft between May and July 1942

Chennault still needed an officer to command the 23rd FG, however, and he found just the man in 34-year-old West Pointer Col Robert L Scott Jr, who was flying transports over the Hump with the Assam-Burma-China Ferry Command from Dinjan. The two men had first met shortly after Scott arrived in theatre in May, the pre-war pursuit pilot convincing Chennault to 'loan' him an AVG P-40E to base at Dinjan, where Scott could use it to patrol the western end of the Hump.

In late June 1942, Scott got the call to move up to Kunming and prepare to take over the 23rd FG. He was still at the latter base working on administrative matters when the group commenced operations in the east on 5 July, so Chennault prevailed on Bob Neale, an AVG holdover who had commanded the 1st PS (and was the top ace in China with 13 victories) to lead the 23rd until Scott arrived.

On the same day that the CATF flew its first fighter mission, 'Tex' Hill lead a flight of nine P-40s from Kunming to Kweilin, where he would assume command of the 75th FS. The squadron was to be based at Hengyang, and amongst Hill's pilots were 'Gil' Bright, 'Ajax' Baumler, four Army lieutenants and a handful of AVG pilots. On that same day, Ed Rector and Charlie Sawyer flew from Hengyang to Kweilin, where the 76th FS would be based. They had an even smaller Army contingent of three lieutenants, plus some more AVG pilots.

Frank Schiel had no such problems with the 74th FS, for his unit boasted a full complement of 18 Army lieutenants at Kunming. However, none of them had been in China more than a few days! As commander of the 'School Squadron', it would be Schiel's responsibility to train these pilots in the art of fighting Chennault-style, whilst at the same time defending Kunming from aerial attack.

The three 23rd FG squadrons took over the aircraft of the AVG units that they replaced, and in the main the P-40s retained the markings of their previous users. For example, most of the 74th's aircraft were Tomahawks of the 3rd PS, so the former's squadron colour, painted in a band around the rear fuselage of its inherited aeroplanes, was red. Similarly, the 75th assumed the white markings of the 1st PS, and the 76th took on the blue of the 2nd PS. These colours remained in effect throughout the P-40's service in the 23rd FG. The squadrons also individually marked

their P-40s in accordance with the AVG system, the 74th using numbers up to 100, the 75th 151 to 199 and the 76th 100 to 150.

Rounding out Chennault's modest fighter force was the aforementioned 16th FS, attached for service from the 51st FG. This unit was supposedly 'loaned' to Chennault for the air defence of Chungking, but its assignment to the nearby base at Peishiyi lasted just a few days – led by Maj Hal Young, the 16th FS moved to Ling Ling on 12 July. Its P-40E-1s were easily distinguishable from the aeroplanes of the remaining three units because they were the only ones displaying the American national marking on their fuselages. The 16th, officially still a unit of the 51st FG, used numbers 11 to 39 to identify its P-40s.

On the morning of 6 July, 'Tex' Hill took off from Kweilin at the head of a flight of four P-40s that were assigned to escort five B-25s sent to bomb an oil refinery at Canton. The tiny formation climbed through a low overcast and headed south toward the target. Fortunately the clouds broke up over Canton, and the medium bombers made their run over the target at 5000 ft. Scoring direct hits on several warehouses along the Pearl River, they then turned for home, but about 30 miles from Canton, one of the B-25 pilots radioed that he was under attack. Hill checked the sky around him to make sure there weren't other enemy fighters lurking in the clouds before he led his flight in a diving attack on the Ki-27s.

'Tex' Hill was already a highly experienced ace, with 9.25 victories to his credit from his time with the AVG, so he had little trouble picking out one of the 'Nates' and firing a telling burst of 0.50-cal 'slugs' into it. The Japanese fighter burst into flames and dove into the ground. Meanwhile, ex-AVG pilot John Petach, leading the second element, engaged three more 'Nates'. He filed this report;

'All three started to turn towards me. I opened fire at 500 yards but was shooting behind the last man so I pulled the nose of my plane well ahead of the EA and gave him a one-second burst. Then the EA pulled into sight right in front of my nose so that my fire raked him as he passed. I saw large holes in his wings, the other two planes started to make a pass at me so I pulled up and took off. I pulled away and saw two more about three miles north of our combat. I turned toward them, and this time they turned away and headed for a mountain. The first plane was just turning around the mountain top when I overhauled the second plane. I gave him about a one-second burst, and he burst into flame and was burning well. Just

Lt Dallas A Clinger was one of the early contingent of pilots who joined the 16th FS/23rd FG straight out of flight school in August 1941. He claimed four victories with the squadron before transferring to the 74th FS in early 1943. His fifth kill took the form of a Ki-43 'Oscar' destroyed on 15 May 1943 during a Japanese raid on Kunming. Like a number of American fighter pilots serving in the CBI, he identified all of his victims (and three probables) as 'Zeros'

All of Dallas Clinger's P-40s carried the *HOLD'N MY OWN* artwork on both sides of their rudders. He flew a P-40E-1 ('White 38') with the 16th FS and a P-40K ('White 48') in the 74th FS. Some personnel in China dubbed the rudder marking the 'Piss on Bissell' in reference to the much-disliked commander of the Tenth Air Force, Maj Gen Clayton Bissell!

then Hill called all planes from combat, so I joined up.'

Hill and Petach were each credited with one 'Nate' destroyed, whilst the latter pilot had his second claim designated as a probable. These were the first victories credited to the 23rd FG, and they were the high point of the CATF's first offensive mission of the war. Sadly, Petach was shot down and killed by ground fire just four days later while leading a dive-bombing attack on the town of Linchuan, which the Japanese were holding. Another AVG pilot, Arnold Shamblin, was also lost on this mission. He reportedly bailed out and was captured by the Japanese, but he did not survive his imprisonment.

1Lt Jack R Best of the 16th FS/23rd FG poses in the autumn of 1942 with his P-40E-1, which was previously assigned to the squadron commander, Maj Harry Young. This combat veteran was later re-numbered 'White 27', and acquired the nickname *Fogarty Fagin III*. Best, who joined the 16th FS in February 1942 during its short stay in Australia, scored one confirmed victory in China

On 19 July the last of the AVG pilots boarded transport aeroplanes at Kunming to begin their long journey home. By that time more Army pilots had been assigned to the 75th and 76th FSs, with Rector's unit at Kweilin, for example, now consisting of 13 pilots, including himself and Sawyer. Ready or not, they now had to carry the load from here on in.

The 23rd FG didn't miss a beat. On 20 July an ailing 'Tex' Hill led a four-aeroplane escort to Kukiang, the P-40s being loaded with six fragmentation bombs under their wings. The pilots dropped them on a troop concentration before strafing a 2000-ton river boat that was later reported to have sunk. Then, on 26 July, the 75th FS sent out seven P-40s to bomb Namchang airfield. Leading this mission was the newly-arrived Maj John Alison, who had transferred in from the 16th FS a week earlier. Alison was a highly experienced aviator with flying time in the USSR, where he had converted communist pilots onto Lend-Lease P-40s.

ON THEIR OWN

During the early weeks in the history of the 23rd FG, the Japanese had established a pattern of sending small formations of bombers over the east

All four of these 75th FS pilots scored victories within a month of their squadron's formation on 4 July 1942. They are, from left, Majs John Alison and David 'Tex' Hill (squadron commander), Capt Albert 'Ajax' Baumler and 2Lt Mack Mitchell. The first three men all became famous aces of the 23rd, whilst Mitchell scored three victories (plus one probable and two damaged) with this unit, and a fourth in 1944 with the 1st Air Commando Group in Burma

China bases at night on harassment missions. At Ling Ling, 16th FS pilots put up with these nuisance raids for as long as they could, but on the night of 26-27 July two of them decided to fight back when three bombers were reported approaching the field.

Future aces Capt Ed Goss and 1Lt John 'Mo' Lombard scrambled in their P-40s at around 0100 hrs, with the former pilot taking off first and quickly spotting the bombers, which were flying with their formation lights on. He made three passes at them over the field and possibly damaged one of the bombers, before they turned off their lights and disappeared into the night. Lombard did not make contact. Later that night Goss scrambled again, this time with another future ace, 1Lt Dallas Clinger, on his wing. The enemy bombers turned back before reaching Ling Ling, and the P-40 pilots returned to base disappointed.

Word of the attempted night interceptions quickly spread throughout the 23rd FG. At Hengyang, John Alison and 'Ajax' Baumler sat down to work out plans for a successful night interception. Their chance to try out their theories came on the night of 29-30 July, the pair taking off at about 0200 hrs following a report of incoming raiders. Alison got away first, passing through a thin layer of haze at 9000 ft. Upon reaching an altitude of 12,000 ft, he commenced circling, his eyes straining in the darkness to pick out the approaching enemy bombers. Soon his radio crackled with the message that bombers had just passed over Hengyang from north to south without attacking. The next message said that they had turned onto a reciprocal course and were heading back north toward the field.

Alison assumed he had missed spotting the bombers because they had passed below the haze layer, but then he had another thought – perhaps they were above him. As he passed over the field he looked up to his left and saw shadows passing against the stars, along with the telltale glow of the bombers' exhaust flames. Alison pulled his P-40 into a climb and called in his sighting to Baumler, who was close by.

As Alison reached 15,000 ft and drew level with his quarry, the twin-engined bombers banked to the right and made a 180-degree turn that would position them for a third run over the field. The turn also placed Alison's P-40 between one of the bombers and the moon, and the tail gunner in the aeroplane to Alison's right opened fire. A stream of tracers caught the P-40 in the nose and stitched it down the length of the fuselage. Alison, not knowing how badly his fighter was damaged, immediately started shooting at the bomber directly in front of him. A two-second burst from his six 0.50-cal guns ripped into the bomber, and it fell away from the formation. He then turned his guns on the bomber to his right that had damaged his P-40, and this time his target burst into flames and fell in pieces from the sky – men on the field at Hengyang saw the exchange of fire, then watched the falling fireball. By this time the engine in Alison's P-40 had begun to smoke, and was throwing oil back over the fighter's windshield.

When Alison launched his attack, Baumler was still several thousand feet below and climbing for all he was worth. He saw the first victim fall away from the other two and decided his best course would be to finish off the damaged machine. After a short chase, he pulled into firing position behind the bomber and cut loose. The bomber staggered as it erupted in flames, before diving into the ground. At this point a gunner in yet

17

another bomber opened fire on Baumler, alerting him to its presence. He chased this aircraft for about 30 miles before catching up with it and blowing it out of the sky.

Alison, meanwhile, was continuing the fight despite his engine running rough, for he could still see the third bomber in the original group he had spotted. He reached firing range just after the aeroplane dropped its bombs, and in the final few seconds before his engine died, he opened fire for the third time. This time his shots must have directly hit the bomber's fuel tanks, because the aeroplane literally exploded. At almost the same moment the engine in Alison's P-40 gasped and quit. He opened the canopy to improve his vision and turned to attempt a dead-stick landing at Hengyang. Just as he began his approach flames belched out from under the engine cowling, momentarily ruining his night vision. Alison duly overshot the airfield, and in his final few seconds of flight, he nursed the P-40 over buildings and trees, before setting it down on the surface of the Hsiang River.

Now it was Baumler's turn to land, but the field at Hengyang remained blacked out. Two members of the 75th FS succeeded in setting out a line of lanterns down each side of the runway, however, and these gave Baumler sufficient light in order to land safely. Alison and Baumler were each awarded two confirmed victories following the mission, and both were later decorated for bravery.

'Ajax' Baumler was in action again shortly after sunrise, for the Japanese sent a mixed force of about 30 fighters – Ki-27 'Nates' and new Ki-43 'Oscars' – back to Hengyang. 'Tex' Hill, 'Gil' Bright and Baumler led a group of P-40s from the 75th and 16th FSs in an attack that took place at 19,000 ft not far from the field. Hill made a head-on pass at a 'Nate' and blew it out of the sky, the Japanese pilot nosing over and diving ground-ward at a dummy P-40 that had been parked on the field at Hengyang. The pilot missed the decoy by about 50 ft, and the 'Nate' buried itself in the ground near the end of the runway.

The air battle raged for about 15 minutes, Bright putting a burst into a Ki-43 from behind that saw it nose over before he had to take evasive action from another 'Oscar' that had got onto his tail. Using his superior speed, the P-40 pilot made a shallow climb and pulled away from the attacker. As this was happening, his wingman followed the first 'Oscar' down and fired more shots into it before the fighter crashed.

Now Bright turned back toward the fight and attempted to position himself behind a Ki-27. However, the 'Nate's' pilot spotted him and made a snap turn that put him in a position for a head-on pass on Bright's P-40. As with Hill's kill just minutes before, the weight of the American's firepower simply shattered the 'Nate', the Japanese fighter pulling up sharply before dropping off in a spin, trailing white smoke. Bright could not stick around to watch the Ki-27 crash though, as he had to evade yet another enemy fighter attempting to attack him. Hill, Bright and Baumler were each credited with one victory apiece, and future ace 1Lt Bob Liles of the 16th FS was awarded a probable for his squadron's first claim of the war.

Enemy fighters returned to Hengyang early the next morning, 31 July, and this time separate P-40 flights from the 75th and 16th FSs met them. Yet another one-sided battle erupted, and three future aces of the 16th –

Edmund Goss, Dallas Clinger and John Lombard – claimed their first victories in the fight. A further three kills were credited to Maj Bright, 1Lt Henry Elias and 2Lt Mack Mitchell of the 75th, and still later that morning Col Scott claimed two victories near Leiyang while flying by himself. In the past 31 hours, the pilots of the 23rd FG had tallied 15 confirmed victories for the cost of just one P-40. Chennault's new boys had met the challenge and were ready for more. This fact was not lost on the Chinese.

Civilian and military leaders at Ling Ling expressed their gratitude to the 16th FS on 1 August by presenting the squadron with a large blue and white banner proclaiming it 'The Great Wall of the Air'. This banner, on which the Great Wall of China was portrayed with a shark's mouth and small yellow wings, became the inspiration for the 16th's squadron badge, and the motif was subsequently painted on the fuselages of most of the unit's P-40s. Similar ceremonies took place in Hengyang to honour the pilots and groundcrews stationed there.

More action followed, but it wasn't until 8 August that the 76th FS scored its first victories. On that day Charlie Sawyer led a four-aeroplane flight out of Kweilin that was tasked with escorting B-25s sent to attack White Cloud airfield at Canton. The following extract taken from the squadron history describes the fight, which began at 1136 hrs;

'As the bombers hit their objective, Lt (Patrick) Daniels peeled off and attacked a flight of three Zeros. He spun out of the turn in his first attack, but recovered with three Zeros on his tail. However, he managed to pull away from them with full throttle. Two of the Zeros fell far behind and turned back; the third Zero followed. Lt Daniels made a quick turn and a head-on run with the Jap. The Zero pilot pulled up to escape the gunfire of the P-40, and to gain position where he could fire on Daniels' canopy from above. Daniels pulled up tightly and saw his tracers from his six 0.50s go through the Zero just as the Jap was about to fire at him. The Zero caught fire and Lt Daniels saw the pilot crawl back on the fuselage of the plane just before it crashed on top of a mountain.

'As the bombers started homeward, Capt Sawyer saw a flight of nine Zeros and I-97s (probably 'Oscars' and 'Nates') coming up to intercept the bombers. He peeled off and headed for the flight. Lt (Charles) DuBois, thinking the flight leader was going down to strafe the airdrome as planned, followed the captain. In the engagement that followed, Capt Sawyer shot down one I-97. Both Capt Sawyer's and Lt Daniels' victories were confirmed.'

Further victories were claimed on 11 and 17 August, but then the reality of war in China set in. Supplies of ammunition and gasoline were running low, the weather was worsening, the P-40s needed servicing and the pilots and groundcrews were suffering from fatigue. Chennault made the decision to pull his units out of east China for the time being, the 16th FS returning to Peishiyi, the 76th joining the 74th at Kunming and the 75th moving to the new base at Chanyi, 50 miles north-east of Kunming.

REACHING OUT

Chennault would shuttle his P-40s in and out of the eastern bases throughout the rest of 1942. Deploying in squadron and even down to flight strength, the pilots would show up at Hengyang, Ling Ling or Kweilin at short notice, fly a couple of missions, and then pull out again for the relative safety of the Kunming area. At the same time, Chennault began to look south into French Indo-China and west into northern Burma for more targets.

Japanese commanders opposing the CATF used high-flying reconnaissance aircraft – primarily twin-engined Ki-46 'Dinahs' – to try to keep track of Chennault's mobile forces, and it was one of these that fell victim to the 74th FS 'School Squadron' at Kunming on 8 September. A single P-40 was sent up to try to intercept the snooper, and Maj Bruce K Holloway, who was serving as 23rd FG operations officer at the time, described the action which ensued in his diary. The entry also provides a look at the CATF's employment of the warning net;

'Started getting plots of one enemy ship around Paoshan about 0845, then another of one plane coming this way from the direction of Hanoi. Regular plots of this plane came up to the 200-km circle and then we got no more. At this point, I sent up one P-40B – No 46, piloted by Lt Thomas R Smith – and gave him instructions to go as high as he could and circle the field. Heard nothing more until about 1000 when Iliang (only 30 km away) reported a dogfight going on overhead. I immediately sent out Lt Daniels in P-40E No 104 to give aid. There were no details given of the dogfight whatsoever over the Chinese net – not even the number of planes involved. However, I considered there was only one enemy plane since it had been pretty definitely one on the plots coming up – therefore I did not alert the command other than putting all pursuit units on station.

'Well, Smith shot him down – a twin-engined I-45 (Ki-45 'Nick'). It was a great day for the 74th, with much rejoicing, which was good for their heretofore rather low state of morale. Smith did one victory roll over the field very low (indication of one plane shot down) and made a very short circle to land. He was so excited he overshot the field and had

Hawk 81-A2 'White 19' (CAF serial P-8146) flew with the AVG's 1st PS prior to its assignment to the 74th FS in July 1942. Note the well-worn red-white-blue pinwheels that are just visible on the hubcaps, and the patches of fresh paint on the fuselage and tail

Hawk 81-A2 'White 59' of the 74th FS came to rest in a drainage ditch after a poor landing by a 'School Squadron' pilot at Kunming in the summer of 1942. After exerting considerable effort, ground-crewmen Orwin and Cotton succeeded in winching the old Tomahawk out of its predicament, and the aeroplane flew again with the name *Yunnan Whore* painted boldly on its engine cowling

One of the most successful pilots in the early days of the 16th FS/23rd FG was Capt Robert E Smith, who is seen here with his P-40E-1 'White 30', which carried the nickname *KatyDid* on its nose. Part of the frontline force in China until early 1943, Smith had scored four victories by the time he returned to America tour-expired. Following a brief rest, he was posted to the P-38-equipped 394th FS as its CO in the autumn of 1943. Part of the 367th FG, the unit was sent to Britain from the USA in the spring of 1944 to serve with the Ninth Air Force, the 394th flying numerous ground attack sorties in the lead-up to the invasion of France on 6 June 1944. The operational tempo was further increased following D-Day, with Smith claiming a Bf 109 damaged on 17 June. Five days later he was killed when his P-38 was shot down by flak near Cherbourg, in France, during yet another strafing mission

to go around again. The first blood for the 74th Squadron, which has been sitting here for two months and had not even seen an enemy plane before today.'

Smith reported he had caught the enemy aircraft at 24,000 ft and pulled in close behind it, firing one burst into the left engine and then five into the right engine, which burst into flames. He was so close behind that oil from the damaged aeroplane sprayed all over the leading edges of the P-40's wings and tail surfaces. Finally, the stricken aircraft nosed over into a long dive and crashed into the ground, giving Thomas Smith his only confirmed victory of the war. Three months later, he was decorated with a Silver Star for the action.

On 25 September the CATF struck Hanoi in force for the first time, nine P-40s, led by Maj Ed Rector of the 76th FS at Kunming, escorting four B-25s sent to attack Gia Lam airfield. The fighters stopped at an auxiliary landing ground at Mengtze, near the Chinese border, en route to top off with fuel. This meant that the fighters could fly back to Kunming without stopping on the return leg of the mission. Rector led the close escort, with Col Bob Scott leading the top cover.

A flight of 13 twin-engined fighters (possibly new Ki-45 'Nicks') were waiting as the Americans approached the target, and they attempted to attack the B-25s. Rector's flight of four was able to cut them off, however, and a swirling fight ensued. Rector himself downed two fighters, and the remaining three members of his flight – 2Lts Pat Daniels, Tim Marks and Howard Krippner – were each credited with one apiece.

After the B-25s had turned for home, Col Scott spotted a flight of three enemy fighters (Ki-45s) climbing towards the retreating bombers. Engaging these aircraft, he later claimed to have shot up all three 'Nicks', and was credited with one confirmed victory and a probable. This took his overall tally to five, making him the first Army pilot to attain ace status within the 23rd FG. By VJ-Day a further 33 pilots would join him on the group's roster of aces.

25 September was also the day that the CATF reported the arrival of 20 new fighter pilots at Kunming, this being the first significant influx of men since the formation of the 23rd FG some three months previous. More importantly, these new pilots had already seen long months of service patrolling and training in the Panama Canal Zone. Although they may not have seen action up to this point in the war, they all knew how to fly and how to shoot. They very quickly learned how to fight Chennault-style too. More good pilots would soon follow from Panama.

The CATF next turned its attention to an even bigger target – the famous port city of Hong Kong. The first mission flown, on 25 October, was a long-planned strike against the docks at Kowloon, which involved seven P-40s of the 75th and 76th FSs and 12 B-25s. Chennault shuttled his attack force into Kweilin early that morning, and the mission to Hong Kong, some 325 miles away, took off at 1130 hrs. The 75th FS unit history gave the following description of the mission;

'The bombers did some good work on the docks and headed for home when a few Zeros appeared. While the Japs were making up their minds on how to hit the bombers, the top cover picked off a few of the Zeros. Maj Hill took his flight into a formation of six Japs. He caught the

Col Robert L Scott, standing at the far right of this photograph with his hands on his hips, watches as groundcrewmen fill a drop tank before attaching it to the belly shackles of his P-40E 'White 7' at Kunming. The Warhawk displays five victory flags beneath the cockpit, which dates this photograph after 25 September 1942, when Scott claimed his fifth victory, and before 25 October, when he was credited with two kills. Scott served as CO of the 23rd FG from 4 July 1942 through to 9 January 1943, finishing his tour with ten kills

first one, Col Scott caught another, Capt Hampshire a third one and Lt Sher of the 76th the fourth. One of the Japs got on the tail of a B-25, and although he was fortunate enough to shoot down the first B-25 in this theatre, his good fortune was immediately followed by bad in the form of Capt Hampshire, who had heard the bomber call for help and had "sandwiched" the Jap and sent him spinning to earth less part of one wing.'

Capt John Hampshire and Lt Morton Sher were two of the new Panama pilots flying their first mission. 1Lt Charles DuBois of the 76th was yet another new Panama pilot to see his first action on this day, although he had to wait until mid-afternoon to intercept a Japanese formation sent to attack Kunming from Indo-China. The six P-40s met a mixed force of Ki-43 'Oscars' and Ki-45 'Nicks' near the border, 30 miles south of Mengtze, and claimed four destroyed and four probables for no losses. DuBois claimed two of the victories, then scored a third kill two days later in a similar encounter over Mengtze.

On 27 November the 23rd FG added three more pilots to its roster of aces during a hastily planned mission to Canton. Originally scheduled as a return bombing raid on Hong Kong, ten B-25s, escorted by 23 P-40s of the 16th, 74th, and 75th FSs, had their target changed the night before the strike due to a strong southerly wind. This headwind, combined with a shortage of 75-gallon drop tanks for the P-40s, forced the switch. Japanese fighters were up in force to oppose the CATF raiders, and a huge air battle developed. The best description of the mission comes from the diary of Maj Holloway of the 76th, who led the top cover flight;

'We came into the target area from the north at 19,000 ft. When about 15 miles from the city, the bombers split into three flights, one to bomb the aircraft factory, one Tien Ho airfield and one any shipping in the river. About the same time they split, Ed Goss (16th FS) ran into about 10 Zeros over to the left, and the fight was on. I didn't take my flight over there, but stayed with the bombers until they got to the targets.

'I stayed with the ones who bombed a ship of about 8000 tons. They made several direct hits on this ship and practically tore it to pieces. Right after this another fight started right under us – Alison got his flight into this one, and by this time the radio conversation was getting good, with everybody yelling for someone else to shoot a Jap off his tail. I heard

Clinger say to (1Lt Jack) Best, "I just knocked one off your tail, but you ought to move over. I almost hit you, too". About this time I saw a parachute descending directly ahead, and since the bombers seemed to be getting away all right, I went on to investigate the parachute, thinking it was a silver-coloured aeroplane in the distance.

'By this time I was right over Tien Ho , so I dived down into the fight. I was really going strong, and my flight really pitched into the middle of it. I made a pass on a Zero and it burst into flames – didn't see it hit the ground but started looking for others. They were all over the place, and you could see tracer bullets going in every direction. I saw burning Japanese aeroplanes falling all over the sky. I made several more runs on Zeros and I-97s and finally got into a good position on an I-97 and gave him a long burst. I don't know whether he went down or not – claimed him as a probable.

'After this I climbed back to about 8000 ft and barged in again. By this time I could see only about three Japs left milling around over the field, like mosquitoes. All the P-40s had either left or were chasing some Jap out over the countryside. The three that were left were very elusive, and I didn't get a good pass at any of them. Finally, two of them got on my tail so I left the vicinity in somewhat of a hurry and started for home. I could hear everybody talking about how many they shot down, and it certainly sounded good.

'I proceeded on toward home all by myself, looking around behind me all the time, when I saw an aeroplane off to my left going back toward Canton. It was a twin-engined light bomber, and was very low over the hills. I turned in behind him and gave chase. Apparently he never did see me. I pulled on up to within about 100 yards behind him, expecting the rear gunner to open up on me at any instant. Either there was no rear gunner, or he was asleep. I opened up from directly astern and poured the lead into him. The whole right side of the plane burst into flames, and immediately thereafter there was an explosion which tore off the entire right wing. The flaming wreckage fell off to the left and crashed into the ground. It made a beautiful fire, and the whole thing took less time than it does to tell about it. I turned around and went home – I didn't have a single bullet hole in my plane.'

When all the claims had been tallied and checked, no fewer than 23 confirmed victories were awarded to the pilots of the 23rd. Only two P-40s were lost, both as a result of running out of fuel on their way home, and both downed pilots returned safely. This single mission tally would remain a group record until war's end.

Capt John Hampshire of the 75th was the top scorer with three confirmed kills, which took his tally to five. Also attaining ace status on this day were 1Lt Charles DuBois of the 76th (two victories) and 1Lt John 'Mo' Lombard of the 16th (one kill). Future aces Maj Bruce K Holloway of the 76th and Capt Goss of the 16th each claimed two apiece, and Lt Col Clinton D 'Casey' Vincent (CATF operations officer), 1Lt Dallas Clinger of the 16th and 1Lt Marvin Lubner of the 76th each got a solitary kill. Finally, Col Scott claimed two fighters to increase his tally to nine.

Eight days later the CATF bade farewell to two of its most successful pilots when Majs 'Tex' Hill and Ed Rector boarded a transport in Kunming to begin their long-awaited journey home. At that time, Hill was the leading active ace in the CBI with 11.75 victories, and Rector wasn't far behind with 6.75 kills. Both men would return to China later in the war to command the 23rd FG.

In a cruel twist of fate, the last active AVG pilot within the CATF, 74th FS commander Frank Schiel, was killed later that same day (5 December) when his Lockheed F-4 Lightning photo-reconnaissance aircraft crashed in bad weather near Suming.

The three new squadron commanders who took over from Hill, Rector and Schiel were Capt 'Ajax'

Baumler (74th FS) and Majs John Alison (75th FS) and Bruce Holloway (76th FS). The final command changes occurred in January 1943 when Col Bob Scott returned to America, his place at the head of the 23rd FG being taken by Bruce Holloway, and control of the 76th FS passing to CATF newcomer, Capt Grant Mahony. Although having only recently

arrived in China, Mahony was no combat novice, having claimed four kills in P-40s over the Philippines and Java in 1941-42, and then spent time with the 51st FG in India

The 23rd FG's last major engagement of 1942 came at Yunnanyi, and involved the 16th FS, which was now under the command of Maj George Hazlett. The unit had deployed to the advanced Hump base near the Burma border on Christmas Eve because Gen Chennault had a hunch that the airfield was due to be attacked by the Japan-

The first pilot to reach ace status in the 76th FS was 1Lt Charles H DuBois (right), whose fourth and fifth kills came on 27 November 1942 over Canton. Sitting with him at Kweilin are fellow pilots Gordon Kitzman (left) and Art Waite. DuBois claimed his sixth, and last, kill on 28 April 1943, by which time he had transferred to the 75th FS. He had flown 87 combat missions, totalling 200+ hours in the cockpit, by the time his tour ended in June 1943

Capt John D 'Mo' Lombard was the first ace of the 16th FS, scoring his fifth victory on 27 November 1942 whilst escorting B-25s sent to bomb Canton. He claimed a further two victories in 1943, and was given command of the 74th FS in February of that year. Lombard was still in charge of the unit when he was killed in a crash in bad weather on 30 June 1943 near Tungting Lake

P-40K 'White 115' was regularly flown by future six-kill ace 1Lt Marvin Lubner of the 76th FS, and it is seen here parked next to a captured A6M2 Zero at Kunming in December 1942. The Mitsubishi fighter was an ex-Tainan Air Group aircraft that had force-landed near Teitsan airfield on 17 February 1941, thus becoming the first example to fall into Allied hands. Subsequently restored to airworthiness by the AVG, the fighter was shipped to the USA in 1943, where it completed in excess of 30 hours of flying. Behind the Zero is a Republic P-43A Lancer, which was assigned to the 76th FS as a hack aircraft

ese. As usual he was right, the enemy catching the 16th on the ground on Christmas afternoon, but fortunately none of its planes was hit. That afternoon, Col Scott flew in from Kunming with orders instructing the 16th FS to prevent any further surprise attacks.

He sent up a two-aeroplane patrol at first light on 26 December, and steadily increased its size throughout the morning. By 1400 hrs the whole squadron was airborne, and just under an hour later

nine twin-engined Japanese bombers, escorted by ten fighters, were spotted overflying the Mekong River from Burma at 17,000 ft. A flight of four P-40s, led by squadron operations officer Maj Hal Pike, were the first to engage the Japanese, and they drew the escorts away from the bombers. Then Col Scott and Maj Hazlett led two more flights in to attack the bombers. One of the participating pilots was Capt Bob Liles, who recalls that his good friend, and fellow 16th FS aviator, Lt Bob Mooney, had been delayed deploying to Yunnanyi, and did not arrive until the day of the fight;

'Just as I was taxying out to take off, I saw Bob Mooney land. I saw him pull his clothes bag out of the plane. He was trying to get refuelled so he could get in on the mission. I left. We were patrolling some miles south of the field, anticipating the Jap attack. Maj Pike was leading my flight, and Hazlett the other. Just as we were about ready to sail into them, a lone aeroplane came streaking up from base, and it was Mooney. I recognised his P-40. He went past me going pretty fast. At that point we went right into these Zeros and bombers.

'I was getting ready to shoot at a Zero, moving to the right. Mooney picked on one going to the left. We never did actually form up as an element and start fighting that way. That was the last time I saw him. He was shot down that day. Most of the Jap planes that came in that day were shot down too. When I landed, someone told me Mooney was down. So I got a Jeep and driver, and we went out west of Yunnanyi to look for him. We knew only approximately where he was – the Chinese told us about the location. So when we got there, I saw him being carried on a door.'

Lt Mooney was still alive when Liles found him, but the young pilot died that night. Another pilot shot down that day was Lt Lewellyn Couch, although he emerged from the experience with only a twisted

Maj Bruce Holloway flies his P-40E over Kunming Lake in late 1942. Holloway took over this aircraft from Maj Ed Rector when he replaced him as CO of the 76th FS in December 1942. 'White 104' was an ex-AVG machine, and it displays a 'flying tiger' decal on its fuselage . Holloway scored his fifth kill in this Warhawk on 14 December 1942, whilst Rector had destroyed a 'Nate' (and claimed a second as a probable) with it the previous 4 July

When Col Scott left China in January 1943, command of the 23rd FG passed to Lt Col Bruce Holloway (left). In turn, Capt Grant Mahony (right) replaced Holloway as CO of the 76th FS. Mahony had scored four kills in the Philippines and Java in 1941-42 before claiming his fifth in China. He was killed in action on 3 January 1945 whilst flying a P-38L with the 8th FG in the Pacific.

knee. On the plus side, the 16th FS was credited with ten victories, and Col Scott added one more to his total. Bob Liles, who would go on to score five victories, and serve as CO of the 16th for more than a year, recorded his first confirmed kill, plus a probable, and Dallas Clinger got his fourth during the mission.

By the end of 1942 the 23rd FG had tallied 97 confirmed victories in six months of combat. The 16th FS led with 35 victories, followed by the 75th and 76th with 29 apiece and the 74th with four.

The first three months of 1943 were relatively quiet in China as the CATF stockpiled supplies at its advance bases, and wedged in missions during sporadic periods of acceptable flying weather. Meanwhile, new P-40K fighters began arriving in greater numbers, and the 23rd FG was able to retire its old AVG Hawks to training units in India.

ENTER THE FOURTEENTH AIR FORCE

As Chennault's forces built up, political forces were at work in Washington DC to place a greater emphasis on the air war in China. The first result of this was the abolishment of the CATF and the creation of the Fourteenth Air Force in its place. This change took place at Kunming on 10 March 1943, Brig Gen Claire Chennault remaining in command of the 'new' organisation. On that day he reported a strength of 103 P-40s, 65 of which were assigned to combat units. The rest were in various states of assembly and repair in local facilities in Kunming. More units would arrive in the coming months, but for the time being the war went on as before for Chennault's pilots.

The quiet period drew to a close in late March 1943 when Chennault deployed his squadrons in preparation for the resumption of offensive operations against the Japanese. He moved the 74th FS, now under the command of Capt John Lombard, to Yunnanyi, where it could protect the Hump corridor and also strike at the Japanese in northern Burma.

Capt Robert L Liles of the 16th FS had just been assigned this new P-40K-5 (42-9912) when he was photographed sitting in it at Chanyi in early 1943. He duly named the aeroplane *Duke*, and continued to fly it well into 1944, by which time he had risen through the ranks to become CO of the 16th. The three kills marked beneath the fighter's cockpit were scored by Liles in December 1942 and January 1943, and he would add a further two victories in September and December to become a 23rd FG ace

Armourers of the 75th FS boresight the guns of P-40K 'White 174' at Kunming in early 1943. Dark green overpainting of the national insignia and the serial number is clearly visible on the fuselage and tail, as is the 11th BS B-25 parked in the background

Sgt Bill Harris of the 75th FS paints a sharksmouth onto a new P-40K at Chanyi in January 1943. Note how he has chalked the outline for the marking, which is now being filled in by hand with a brush and a paint pallet. Drawn on without the use of a template, no two sharksmouths were the same

Groundcrewmen from the 75th FS take a break from refuelling aircraft on the flightline at Hengyang. The P-40K at left is fitted with mounting brackets for small bombs beneath its wing. Note also that the outline for the shark's tongue has been chalked on, although it has not yet been painted, and that neither P-40K has a shark's eye on its nose

The 16th FS, led by new CO Maj Hal Pike, and one flight of the 76th FS went to Kweilin, and the 75th moved to nearby Ling Ling. From these bases, they could hit the Japanese in the Hankow and Canton/Hong Kong areas. Meanwhile, the bulk of the 76th remained at Kunming for air defence and offensive missions into Indo-China.

The month of April was an all-75th FS show, and one of the legendary figures of the China air war emerged during this time. Capt John Hampshire scored his sixth victory on 1 April 1943 over Ling Ling, and claimed two more kills 23 days later to take the scoring lead among active pilots in the CBI. He described the latter action in a letter to his father back home in Grants Pass, Oregon, on 25 April. Hampshire wrote;

'Yesterday the Japanese paid us another visit, and it was a dilly. They really sent in the first team this time, and they had the most beautiful air discipline I have ever seen. There were 30 or so of them, all fighters, and it was impossible to catch anyone asleep or by themselves, so it was mighty tough going for awhile. When the smoke cleared, we had shot down five, and we didn't lose any. So it wasn't a bad day, although it certainly could have been better. The fight was a fairly long one, and just when it was end-

27

ing, one of their twin-engined fighters flew over and dropped out a
bunch of pamphlets' (the pamphlet
challenged the American air forces
to a 'decisive air battle').

'The monkey that dropped the
pamphlets ran into a little hard luck
on the way home. For a while it
looked like I'd never catch him, but
I finally did after chasing him a hun-
dred miles. So that ended the show for that day. I got two.'

The Japanese turned the tables the day after Hampshire wrote the
letter. At Yunnanyi, a breakdown in the warning net near the Salween
River allowed a force of enemy bombers and fighters to catch Lombard's
74th FS on the ground on 26 April, putting the unit temporarily out of
action. The 16th and 75th FSs pulled back to Yunnanyi and Kunming
respectively from their eastern bases, as further trouble was expected.
That trouble arrived on 28 April, but this time the Japanese target was
Kunming, which hadn't been bombed in daylight since the first AVG
mission of 20 December 1941. The enemy bombers managed to reach
Kunming and bomb the field, but they paid a high price at the hands of
the 75th on their way home. Again, the warning net had failed to give
sufficient notice of the raid, so Lt Col John Alison led his squadron on an
interception course that would allow the P-40s to catch the Japanese
during their return flight to Burma.

The 23rd FG's tally for the mission was 11 confirmed and eight probables, with Capt Hollis Blackstone of the 75th being credited with two
destroyed and one probable. Another notable scorer was Maj Ed Goss,
who had transferred to the 75th from the 16th in preparation for assum-
ing command of the squadron from Alison. Goss's single victory brought
his total to five. Future aces scoring in the fight included Roger Pryor and
Joe Griffin, who claimed one fighter apiece, while Charles DuBois of the
76th scored his sixth, and last, victory in the fight and Hampshire
increased his tally to 11 confirmed with two kills.

John Hampshire's luck ran out four days later. By then, the 75th had
moved back to Ling Ling and was preparing to resume offensive
operations. On 2 May the Japanese
beat them to the punch by sending a
large force of fighters from the 25th
and 33rd Sentais down from Hankow to attack the base. Lt Col Alison
scrambled 16 P-40s to challenge
them, and the two formations met
not far from the airfield. Records
conflict on the exact sequence of
events, but it appears that 1Lt Don
Brookfield scored a victory in the
initial engagement, and then the
P-40s began chasing the enemy back
toward Hankow. Japanese fighters
continued to fall on the flight north,

Seen at Chanyi in early 1943, these
two P-40Ks each display a 'full set'
of 16th FS unit markings. Lt George
Barnes was the pilot of 'White 24',
which was named *Thunderbird II*,
and Lt C D Griffin flew 'White 26'.
Note the 'Flying Wall of China'
squadron badge forward of the
individual aircraft number, white
star hubcaps and four victory flags
on Barnes' P-40 – he finished his
tour with four aircraft confirmed
destroyed and one probable. The
Warhawk's serial number (42-46263)
has been crudely painted out on the
tail, which was standard practice in
China

On 28 April 1943 a strong force of
Japanese bombers attacked the
airfield at Kunming, killing several
American personnel and shattering
the control tower, seen here.
Defending P-40 pilots of the 23rd FG
were credited with shooting down
11 of the raiders

Crewchief Don Van Cleve poses with *HELLZAPOPPIN* (P-40K 'White 162'), which he serviced in 1942-43 whilst assigned to the 75th FS. Its regular pilot was 1Lt Joseph H Griffin, who scored three victories in China and four flying P-38Js with the 393rd FS/367th FG in the ETO in 1944. Note the white fuselage band and red-white-blue pinwheels on the hubcaps. The solitary victory marking beneath the cockpit signifies Griffin's first confirmed kill (an unidentified bomber, possibly a Ki-48), scored on 23 November 1942 over Kweilin

These seven pilots from the 75th FS combined to score 11 victories when Japanese bombers raided Kunming on 28 April 1943. Sitting on the aeroplane, from left to right, are Maj Ed Goss, Lt Col John Alison and 1Lt Roger Pryor. Standing, from left to right, are 1Lts Joe Griffin and Mack Mitchell and Capts John Hampshire and Hollis Blackstone. *KING BOOGIE* was the P-40K assigned to 1Lt William 'Beel' Grosvenor, who would score five victories, three probables and three damaged during his combat tour in China

Capt John Hampshire poses with his P-40K-1 'White 161' (42-45732) at Ling Ling in early April 1943, by which time his score stood at six confirmed. He would add seven more victories, and tie with AVG ace Bob Neale as the top-scoring American P-40 pilot of the war, before being killed in action in this aeroplane on 2 May 1943. In 1998 the airport at Grants Pass, Oregon (Hampshire's hometown), was renamed in his honour

with Hampshire getting two near Changsha. Alison wrote a description of what happened next in a letter to Hampshire's father;

'When it was over, Johnny rejoined my formation, and as he pulled in close on my wing I could see a big grin on his face. He told me on the radio that he had followed his man down and saw him crash and burn. We then headed north and after a very long chase intercepted a formation of Jap fighters which had been strafing a Chinese town. It must have been a lucky shot from a Zero that got him, as none of us saw it happen. John set his plane down in a river and the Chinese took him to the nearest hospital. He died before he could reach adequate medical attention.'

Hampshire had crashed near a Chinese army outpost, which quickly relayed word back to Ling Ling that the pilot was wounded but alive. The 75th FS flight surgeon, Capt Ray Spritzler, told Alison he wanted to fly to the crash site and

29

see if he could help Hampshire. When Lt Joe Griffin volunteered to fly Spritzler there in the baggage compartment of a P-43, Alison reluctantly agreed. The flight surgeon planned to bail out of the aeroplane over the crash site. Shortly after the P-43 took off, the Chinese relayed another message: Hampshire had died. Alison tried unsuccessfully to recall Griffin by radio, but bad weather forced the P-43 to land at an unmanned airstrip near a Chinese village. Griffin and Spritzler returned to Ling Ling the next morning. Joe Griffin scored three victories in China and then four more in the ETO during 1944 while serving as a squadron commander in the 367th FG.

Hampshire's two kills on 2 May gave him a total of 13 confirmed victories, tying him with Bob Neale of the AVG as the top-scoring American P-40 ace of the war. One more pilot, 23rd FG commander Col Bruce Holloway, would join them at the top of the pile.

THE BUILD-UP BEGINS

The first step in the build-up of the Fourteenth Air Force was the addition of a heavy bomber unit in the form of the 308th BG. Equipped with B-24D Liberators, the 308th flew its first mission from Kunming on 4 May 1943 when it attacked Samah Bay on Hainan Island in the South China Sea. The B-24s encountered light flak and no Japanese fighters over the target. Four days later the Liberators joined B-25s of the 11th BS and 24 P-40s of the 16th and 75th FSs in a strike against Canton. The complex mission plan called for the long-range B-24s to fly to the target directly from Kunming, while the rest of the strike force would stage through Kweilin and meet them just prior to reaching the target area.

The mission went according to plan and caught the Japanese at Canton by surprise. Enemy fighters were spotted taking off from White Cloud airfield during the attack, so the P-40s stayed in the area to hold them off while the bombers withdrew. A wild 20-minute air battle ensued, and when it was over 23rd FG pilots tallied 13 'Oscars' and 'Nates' destroyed, plus five probables. Among the victors was 1Lt Jim Little of the 75th FS, whose solitary 'Oscar' kill raised his overall tally to five victories. The new ace would score twice more a week later, and then be forced to wait seven years before getting another chance. On 27 June 1950, Little claimed one of the first kills of the Korean War when he shot down a North Korean La-7 fighter while flying an F-82G Twin Mustang (see *Aircraft of the Aces 4 - Korean War Aces* for further details).

In addition, Lt Col Alison was credited with his fifth kill. He would soon leave China for an important new assignment to help form the 1st Air Commando Group, but like Little, he would first add to his score.

The 23rd FG shuffled its fighter squadrons on 11 May, moving the 74th and 76th FSs to eastern bases at Ling Ling and Kweilin, while pulling back the 75th FS to Kunming and putting the 16th at Yunnanyi. By 15 May the 75th was settled at Kunming, and the 74th FS was at Chanyi, waiting for the base at Kweilin to be prepared for its arrival. The warning net came alive that morning with reports of a large enemy force approaching Kunming from Burma, and at 0910 hrs Col Holloway led a patrol out to look for the raiders.

The three P-40s were 60 miles from base and cruising at 23,000 ft when Holloway looked up to see a massive (for China) force of 30 Ki-48 'Lily'

Mechanics of the 75th FS change a tyre on the P-40K assigned to 1Lt James W Little at Ling Ling in the spring of 1943. Distinctive markings visible in this photograph include Little's name and two victory flags beneath the cockpit, a white band on the rear fuselage (forward of which was painted a white 152) and black US ARMY titling under the wings. Note that the shark's eye was still lacking detail when this shot was taken. 'Poco' Little scored seven victories with the 75th between January and May 1943, and added an eighth kill to his tally in the opening phase of the Korean War on 27 June 1950 when he downed a North Korean La-7 whilst flying an F-82 Twin Mustang

bombers approaching at 26,000 ft, escorted by 23 Ki-43 'Oscars' of the 64th Sentai stepped up above them at 30,000 ft. Holloway began to climb as he called in the raid to Kunming, ordering Maj Ed Goss to scramble his 75th FS to help with the impending interception.

Holloway, with Maj Roland Wilcox and Lt Charles Crysler on his wing, clawed his way to 28,000 ft and turned in behind the formation to attack the escorts. By that time the 'Lilys' were making their run over Kunming airfield, but fortunately their bombs went wide and did little damage.

In the ensuing engagement the P-40 pilots claimed to have destroyed 16 aircraft, with a further nine as probables, without loss. One of those definitely shot down was 64th Sentai 'Oscar' pilot Lt Takeshi Endo, commander of the 3rd Chutai (see *Aircraft of the Aces 13 - Japanese Army Air Force Aces 1937-45* for further details). As a result of the action, the 23rd FG added yet another ace to its growing list when Capt Dallas Clinger of the 74th FS made contact with the fleeing Japanese formation at the end of the battle. He claimed one 'Oscar' destroyed, plus a probable, and these were the first successes attributed to a 74th FS pilot in 1943. Following the completion of the 74th's move to Kweilin on 19 May, its pilots would get plenty of opportunity to add to their scores.

In early May 1943, Japanese ground forces at Hankow commenced a campaign with hopes of taking China out of the war. In a two-pronged attack, one force headed westward up the Yangtze River toward Chungking, while the other moved south from Tungting Lake along the Hsiang River, its objective being to capture the tactically important Fourteenth Air Force airfields at Hengyang, Ling Ling and Kweilin. Neither thrust was destined to succeed thanks in part to the work of the 74th and 76th FSs, which flew in support of Chinese forces at Changsha.

P-40K 'White 111' was the mount of 76th FS CO Maj Grant Mahony during the spring of 1943. Photographed whilst having its guns boresighted at Ling Ling, the Warhawk displays an unusual mix of markings, including an AVG flying tiger on the fuselage and twin white command stripes encircling the fin and rudder. Mahony scored his fifth victory with this fighter, over Ichang, on 23 May 1943

The two squadrons, organised as the East China Task Force under the control of Col Casey Vincent, commenced offensive operations against the advancing Japanese as soon as the enemy launched its offensive. On 23 May, Maj Lombard led two flights of his 74th FS from Kweilin to the advanced base at Hengyang. On that same day, Maj Grant Mahony became an ace when he led nine 76th FS P-40s on a strafing mission to the town of Ichang, on the banks of the Yangtze River north-west of Tungting Lake. The major encountered a single Ki-27 'Nate' en route to the target and quickly shot it down. He also destroyed a further two Ki-27s on the airfield at Ichang, and his flight shot up four trucks and a fuel dump.

The aggressive Maj Mahony would leave for home on 9 June following 19 months in combat. He returned to the CBI to fly with John Alison in the 1st Air Commando Group, then began a third tour in the Pacific Theatre late in the war. Promoted to lieutenant colonel, Mahony joined the P-38L-equipped 8th FG in the Philippines in mid-December 1944 and was shot down and killed by ground fire during a strafing mission on 3 January 1945.

The fighting continued in east China throughout June 1943, and as the 23rd FG approached its first birthday, the unit suffered the loss of one of its top aces. On the morning of 20 June, Maj John Lombard set out from Hengyang to check weather conditions north of Tungting Lake, but the seven-victory ace was caught under a dropping overcast and crashed into a mountainside near Yiyang. He died one day short of his 24th birthday.

The weather was bad all over China on 4 July 1943 (the first anniversary of the 23rd FG), the 74th FS hostel nearly flooding in a torrent of rain at Kweilin. Ignoring the precipitation, the men of the 75th FS enjoyed an extra egg for breakfast and a glass of 'Sham-Shu' (local Chinese 'firewater') with their dinners. Throughout the group, men had time to reflect on their successes over the past year: They had held the line against the Japanese in east China while protecting their end of the Hump from enemy attack, scoring 171 confirmed victories in the process.

On the other hand, nothing much had changed for the better, either. The older P-40s had given way to newer K- and M-models, but the aeroplanes were still few in number and well past their best. Fuel and ammunition remained in short supply, not to mention luxuries such as fresh meat, soap and uniforms. Even worse, mail deliveries from home were sporadic at best.

In Kunming, Col Bruce Holloway tried to make light of the situation in his typical droll manner during a first anniversary party staged for 23rd FG personnel. 'A year earlier, when the unit was activated', he noted, 'there wasn't a single American magazine at Kunming for the guys to read. Now there were several'.

Nobody laughed.

COLOUR PLATES

1
Hawk 81-A2 CAF serial P-8194/'White 7' of Robert H
Neale, 23rd FG HQ, Kweilin, China, July 1942

2
P-40E (serial unknown) 'White 104' of Maj Edward F
Rector, CO of the 76th FS/23rd FG, Kweilin, China,
4 July 1942

3
Hawk 81-A2 CAF serial P-8156/'White 46' of 1Lt Thomas R
Smith, 74th FS/23rd FG, Kunming, China, September 1942

4
P-40E (serial unknown) 'White 7' of Col Robert L
Scott, CO of the 23rd FG, China, September 1942

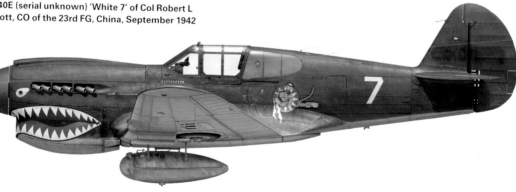

5
P-40E-1 41-36402/'White 38' of 1Lt Dallas A Clinger,
16th FS/23rd FG, Kweilin, China, Autumn 1942

6
P-40K-1 42-46263/'White 24' of 1Lt George R Barnes,
16th FS/23rd FG, Chanyi, China, Spring 1943

7
P-40K-1 42-45232/'White 161' of Capt John F Hampshire Jr,
75th FS/23rd FG, China, Spring 1943

8
P-40K (subtype and serial unknown) 'White 162' of 1Lt Joseph H
Griffin, 75th FS/23rd FG, China, Spring 1943

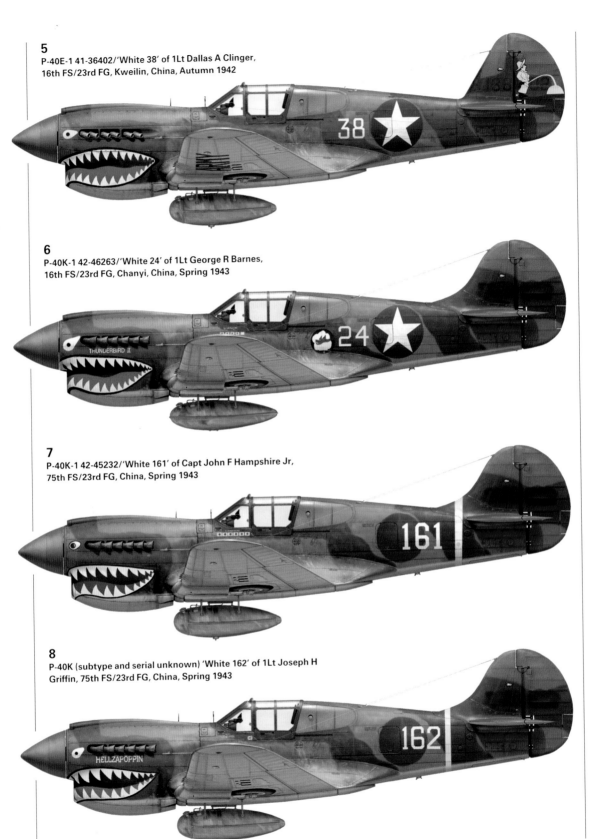

9
P-40K (subtype and serial unknown) 'White 152' of 1Lt James
W Little, 75th FS/23rd FG, China, Spring 1943

10
P-40K-1 42-45911/'White 111' of Maj Grant Mahony,
CO of the 76th FS/23rd FG, China, Spring 1943

11
P-40K (subtype and serial unknown) 'White 115' of 1Lt Marvin
Lubner, 76th FS/23rd FG, China, Summer 1943

12
P-40K-5 (serial unknown) 'White 1' of Col Bruce K
Holloway, CO of the 23rd FG, China, August 1943

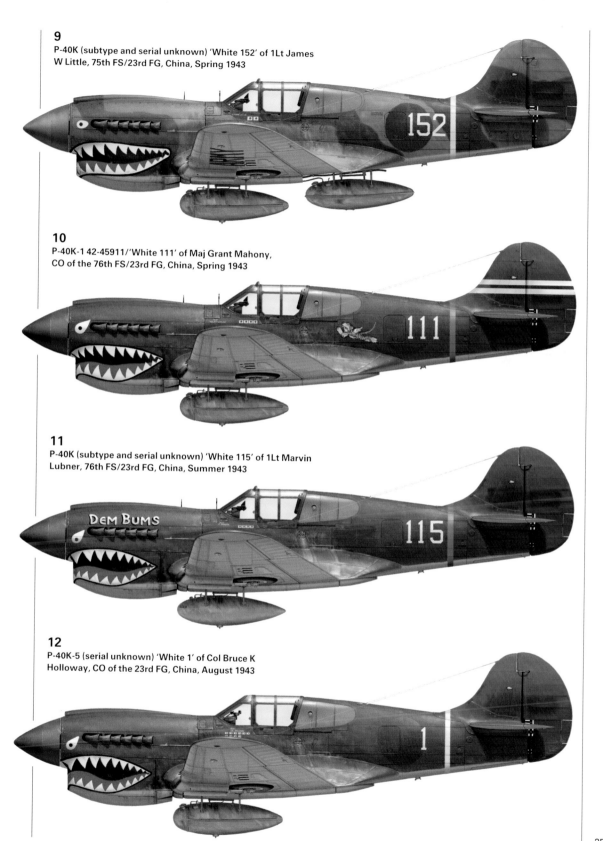

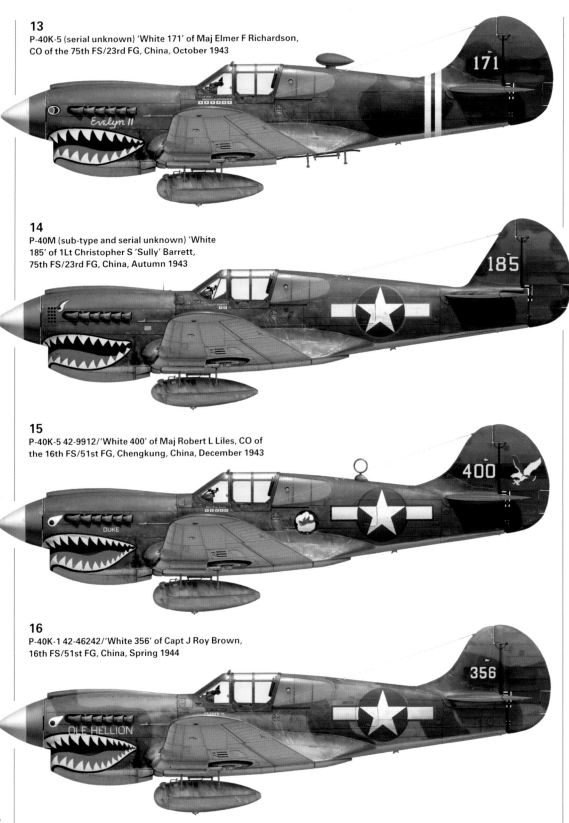

13
P-40K-5 (serial unknown) 'White 171' of Maj Elmer F Richardson,
CO of the 75th FS/23rd FG, China, October 1943

14
P-40M (sub-type and serial unknown) 'White
185' of 1Lt Christopher S 'Sully' Barrett,
75th FS/23rd FG, China, Autumn 1943

15
P-40K-5 42-9912/'White 400' of Maj Robert L Liles, CO of
the 16th FS/51st FG, Chengkung, China, December 1943

16
P-40K-1 42-46242/'White 356' of Capt J Roy Brown,
16th FS/51st FG, China, Spring 1944

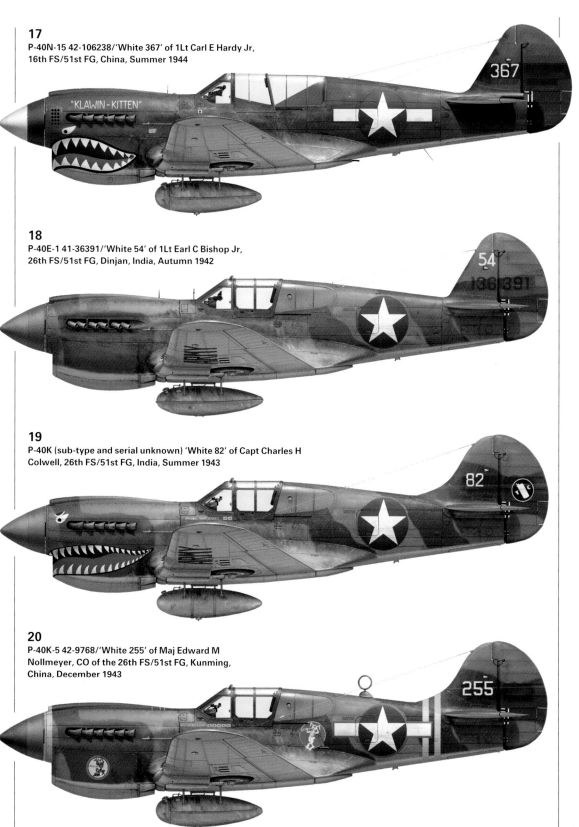

17
P-40N-15 42-106238/'White 367' of 1Lt Carl E Hardy Jr,
16th FS/51st FG, China, Summer 1944

18
P-40E-1 41-36391/'White 54' of 1Lt Earl C Bishop Jr,
26th FS/51st FG, Dinjan, India, Autumn 1942

19
P-40K (sub-type and serial unknown) 'White 82' of Capt Charles H
Colwell, 26th FS/51st FG, India, Summer 1943

20
P-40K-5 42-9768/'White 255' of Maj Edward M
Nollmeyer, CO of the 26th FS/51st FG, Kunming,
China, December 1943

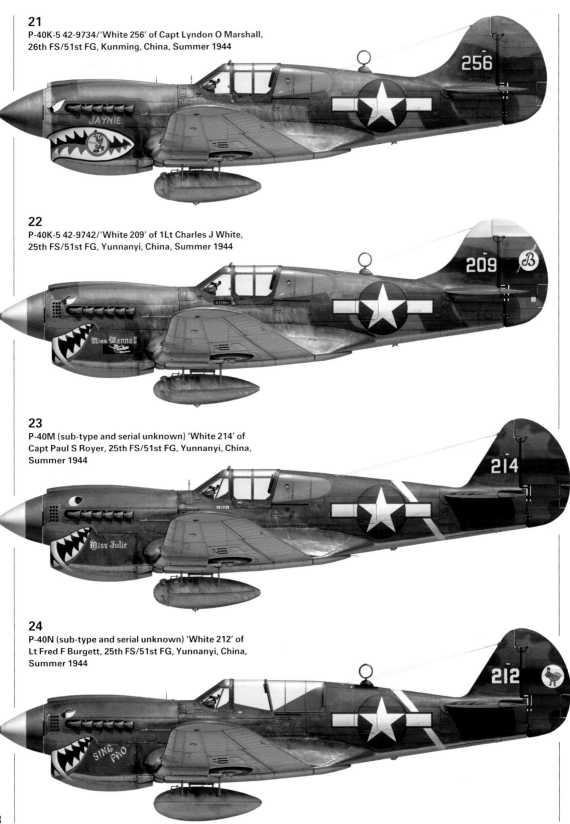

21
P-40K-5 42-9734/'White 256' of Capt Lyndon O Marshall,
26th FS/51st FG, Kunming, China, Summer 1944

22
P-40K-5 42-9742/'White 209' of 1Lt Charles J White,
25th FS/51st FG, Yunnanyi, China, Summer 1944

23
P-40M (sub-type and serial unknown) 'White 214' of
Capt Paul S Royer, 25th FS/51st FG, Yunnanyi, China,
Summer 1944

24
P-40N (sub-type and serial unknown) 'White 212' of
Lt Fred F Burgett, 25th FS/51st FG, Yunnanyi, China,
Summer 1944

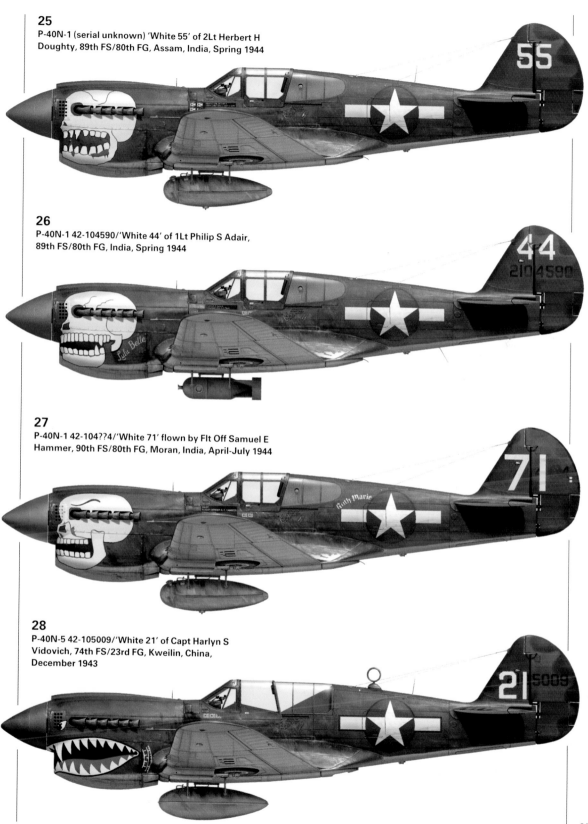

25
P-40N-1 (serial unknown) 'White 55' of 2Lt Herbert H
Doughty, 89th FS/80th FG, Assam, India, Spring 1944

26
P-40N-1 42-104590/'White 44' of 1Lt Philip S Adair,
89th FS/80th FG, India, Spring 1944

27
P-40N-1 42-104??4/'White 71' flown by Flt Off Samuel E
Hammer, 90th FS/80th FG, Moran, India, April-July 1944

28
P-40N-5 42-105009/'White 21' of Capt Harlyn S
Vidovich, 74th FS/23rd FG, Kweilin, China,
December 1943

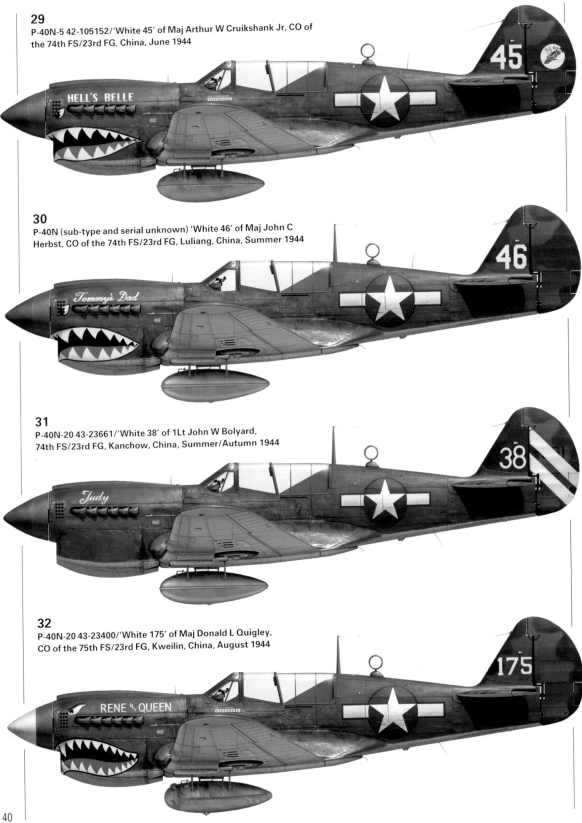

29
P-40N-5 42-105152/'White 45' of Maj Arthur W Cruikshank Jr, CO of
the 74th FS/23rd FG, China, June 1944

HELL'S BELLE

30
P-40N (sub-type and serial unknown) 'White 46' of Maj John C
Herbst, CO of the 74th FS/23rd FG, Luliang, China, Summer 1944

Tommy's Dad

31
P-40N-20 43-23661/'White 38' of 1Lt John W Bolyard,
74th FS/23rd FG, Kanchow, China, Summer/Autumn 1944

Judy

32
P-40N-20 43-23400/'White 175' of Maj Donald L Quigley,
CO of the 75th FS/23rd FG, Kweilin, China, August 1944

RENE 'n' QUEEN

33
P-40N-20 43-23266/'White 194' of 1Lt Donald S Lopez,
75th FS/23rd FG, Kweilin, China, July 1944

34
P-40N (sub-type and serial unknown) 'White 165' of
1Lt Forrest F Parham, 75th FS/23rd FG, Kanchow,
China, Autumn 1944

35
P-40N-5 42-105427 (CAF serial P-11139)/'White 646' of
Maj William L Turner, CO of the CACW's 32nd FS/3rd FG,
Kweilin, China, Spring 1944

36
P-40N-20 CAF serial P-11461/'White 660' of Lt Col William N Reed,
CO of the CACW's 7th FS/3rd FG, Liangshan, China, August 1944

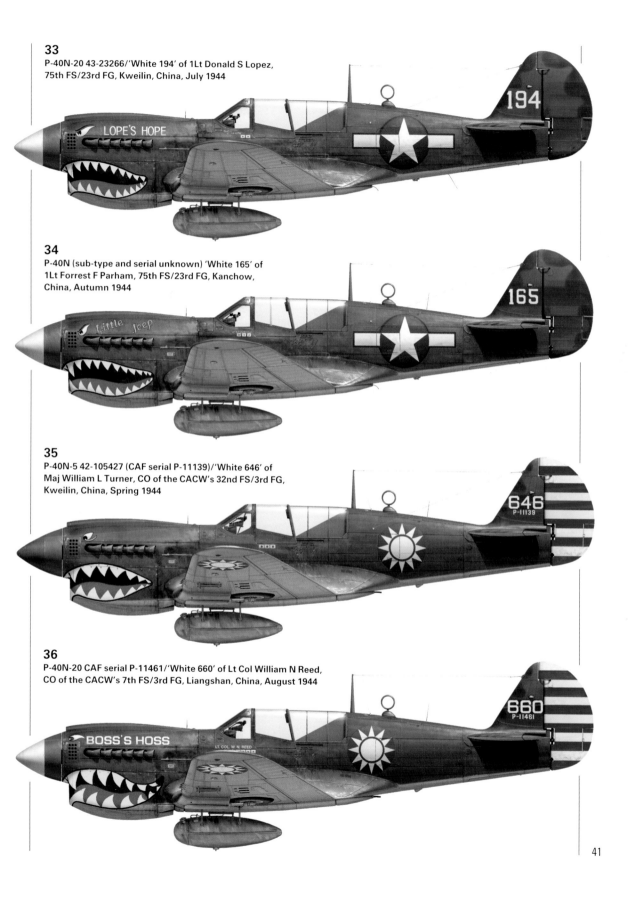

37
P-40N-5 CAF serial P-11151/'White 663' of Capt Wang Kuang Fu,
CACW's 7th FS/3rd FG, Laohokow, China, January 1945

38
P-40N-15 CAF serial P-11249/'White 681' of Capt Raymond L
Callaway, CACW's 8th FS/3rd FG, Liangshan, China, August 1944

39
P-40N (sub-type and serial unknown) 'Black 726' of
Col John A Dunning, CACW's 5th FG HQ, Chihkiang,
China, Summer/Autumn 1944

40
P-40N (sub-type and serial unknown) 'Black 767' of Capt
William K Bonneaux, CACW's 17th FS/5th FG, Chihkiang,
China, Summer/Autumn 1944

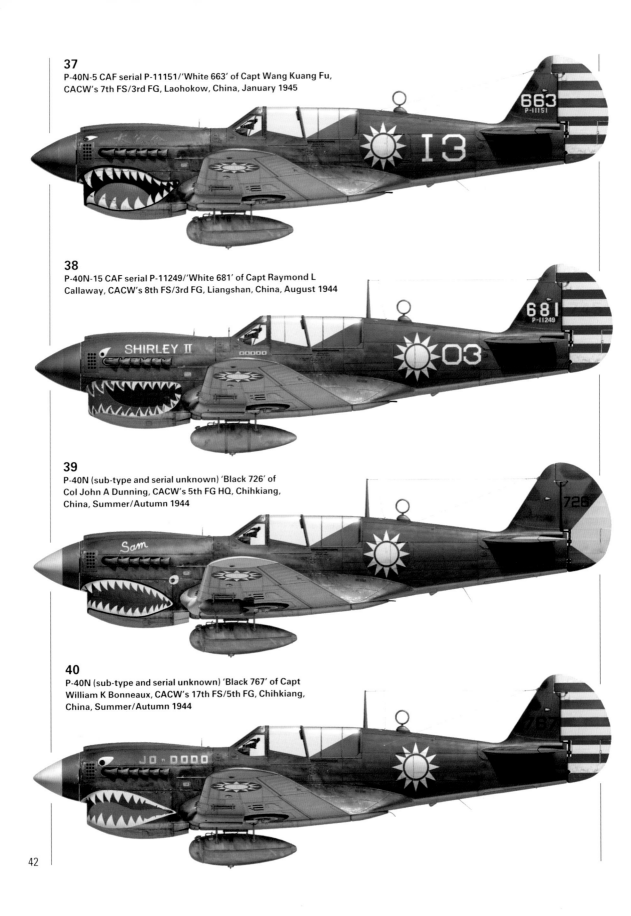

JUNGLE FIGHTERS

The United States Army Transport *President Coolidge* slipped away from its dock in San Francisco harbour on the afternoon of 12 January 1942 and headed out to sea. Joined by two other transport ships and a Navy cruiser, the *Coolidge* became part of the first convoy carrying American troops to leave the mainland of the United States following the declaration of war against Japan.

Among the troops on board the *Coolidge* were 53 officers and 894 enlisted men assigned to the 51st Pursuit Group, US Army Air Corps. The 51st was barely a year old, having formed at Hamilton Field, California, in January 1941 with three squadrons, the 16th, 25th and 26th. Under the command of an aggressive 37-year-old major, Homer L 'Tex' Sanders, the 51st grew rapidly during the year, and its pilots soon became proficient with the Curtiss P-40 fighter. When war broke out, Sanders was quick to declare his unit combat-ready. Soon thereafter one wag in the 51st, having noted the growing fame of the AVG in China, nicknamed his unit 'Homer's Volunteer Group', and it stuck.

Two other Army pursuit groups, the 35th and 49th, also were in the convoy, which headed south across the Pacific Ocean toward Australia. The passage was uneventful, and on 1 February the ships reached Melbourne. After a short stay, during which the 49th parted company and 16 new pilots joined the 51st, the two remaining fighter groups moved on to Fremantle, Western Australia.

The war was going badly for the United States at this time. In Java, US Army fighter units desperately needed reinforcements, so 32 P-40Es were craned aboard the aeroplane tender USS *Langley* and 25 more unassembled Warhawks stuffed into crates and loaded onto the freighter *Sea Witch*. The personnel of the 51st FG, along with a further ten crated Warhawks, boarded the USS *Holbrook*, and the convoy departed Fremantle on 23 February with its destination unknown to all but a few personnel. Soon the *Langley* and *Sea Witch* left the convoy and headed for Java, but they never made port, for Japanese bombers attacked the aeroplane tender off the coast and sank it with five direct hits.

The *Holbrook*, meanwhile, proceeded across the Indian Ocean to Colombo, Ceylon (now Sri Lanka), and then on to Karachi, in Pakistan. When the 51st FG disembarked at the latter port on 12 March 1942, no one could have guessed that another six months would pass before the unit was finally ready to engage the enemy at full strength.

The 51st FG was assigned to the Tenth Air Force, which had been formed in February 1942 to support the Chinese in their fight

One of the first aircraft lost at Karachi was P-40E 'White 14' (41-5635) of the 16th FS, which crashed on 28 March 1942 after its engine quit on take-off with 2Lt Edward LaCour at the controls. Note the red-centred pre-war national insignia on the fighter's fuselage. LaCour would die two months later in a second P-40 crash

against Japan. However, a fighter group can not achieve much with only ten aeroplanes and a short roster of pilots. Despite their paucity in numbers, the P-40s were nevertheless assembled in the huge R.101 dirigible hangar at Camp Malir, and the pilots commenced a limited schedule of proficiency flying. This boring existence continued until May when 68 reinforcement aircraft (and pilots, led by Lt Col John E Barr) flew off the carrier USS *Ranger* on the 10th of that month whilst it steamed along the coast of West Africa. The P-40s were bound for Karachi.

Over the next two weeks the pilots would traverse the African continent and the Middle East on their way to Camp Malir. Among their ranks were a number of future aces, including Lts Arthur W Cruikshank, Edmund R Goss, Robert L Liles, and Edward M Nollmeyer. The Warhawks (mostly P-40E-1s, with a few P-40K-1s) were described as being in 'sad shape' by the time they arrived in Karachi, and groundcrews were kept busy restoring them to full operability. With all the P-40s now safely in Karachi, the 51st FG at last began to resemble a fighter group.

STARTING SMALL

In keeping with the Tenth Air Force mission, the 51st FG was called on to send one fighter squadron to China as the disbandment date of the AVG approached. Accordingly, the 16th FS departed for Kunming on 22 June for detached service with the 23rd FG. The next day three experienced pilots from the 26th FS were ordered to Dinjan, in Assam, in order to perform reconnaissance flights over Burma. The pilots chosen for this task were Capt Thrashley M 'Andy' Hardy and 1Lts Jack G Hamilton and John 'Swede' Svenningson. No ground personnel were sent, the pilots instead being responsible for servicing and arming their own aircraft. Jack Hamilton recalled the experience in a letter to the author;

'The ranking officer in charge was a Col Boatner. There were three old P-40Bs at Dinjan. We could never get more than one flying at the same time, and two had to be cannibalised to keep one flying. It was monsoon time, and heavy weather would come up rather quickly. At first we just flew locally to get adjusted to the weather, learning landmarks along the Brahmaputra River and mountain peaks for orientation. We each made a flight like this before we undertook to fly over northern Burma. We lived in one of the tea planter's houses and slept on Army cots with mosquito nets. Our food was prepared by some local inhabitants, as I recall.

'At that early time I don't think there were more than a dozen DC-3s flying the Hump. The China National Air Corporation (CNAC) was there, but I also recall some former airline pilots who had been called to Air Corps active duty. I think Dinjan was the only operational airfield there in June 1942 – Chabua was beginning to be built.

Capt Edward M Nollmeyer (left) and Lt George Grammas of the 26th FS relax next to the alert shack at one of the Assam bases. Nollmeyer destroyed two Japanese aircraft when stationed in India, and went on to become his unit's premier ace. His first assigned aircraft was P-40E-1 'White 95'. Grammas completed his combat tour without registering an aerial victory

The 26th FS's 1Lt Jack Hamilton was one of the first three USAAF pilots sent to Dinjan, in Assam, in late June 1942 to perform reconnaissance flights over Burma. No groundcrewmen accompanied them, which meant that the pilots were responsible for servicing and arming their own aircraft. Here, Hamilton poses with his P-40K, 'White 80', in the spring of 1943

'"Andy", "Swede" and I rotated solo reconnaissance missions over northern Burma until 8 July 1942. On that date it was "Andy's" turn to fly. I went out to the plane with him, and remember standing on the wing and wishing him luck just before he took off. He was never seen or heard from again. After four hours, when he didn't return, I was in the office berating the Army for making us fly these missions alone. We thought we should have two planes to go on these missions. Col Boatner was in the office and heard my complaints. He came out of his office and really chewed me out – threatened to court martial me if he heard any more remarks like I had been making. "Swede" and I went in to Dibrugarh and paid $85 for a fifth of Scotch and proceeded to dispense with it.

'In a few days, Roy Santini and Stanley Combs came to Dinjan with two P-40s from Karachi. We also had an Allison engine representative – Arne Butteberg – come over (the Hump) from Kunming to try to help us get the Allison engines running well.'

Jack Hamilton, who eventually became commander of a flight of P-40s based at Lilibari (a sod field on the north side of the Brahmaputra River), flew 50 missions over enemy territory before returning home in 1943.

In Karachi, the 25th and 26th FSs continued to mark time through the summer of 1942 until orders finally arrived in mid-September for the latter unit to move up to Dinjan. The full squadron complement of 30 P-40s was in place at the 26th's new base by 1 October, where it shared facilities with the 51st FG Headquarters. Two flights from the 25th FS had moved into the new satellite base at Sookerating by the end of the month, although they arrived too late to participate in the 51st FG's first clashes with the enemy.

DEFENDING THE HUMP

Japanese reconnaissance aircraft had been keeping an eye on the build-up at Dinjan, and on 19 October 1Lt Alvin B Watson of the 26th FS scrambled in an attempt to intercept a Ki-46 'Dinah' that was approaching the base. Climbing as rapidly as possible, Watson caught up with his prey about 40 miles south of Margherita and fired a long burst into it. The 'Dinah' quickly caught fire and crashed into the jungle, thus giving the 51st FG its first confirmed victory of the war.

A week later, the Japanese caught the group totally by surprise when 96 bombers and fighters appeared over Dinjan without warning. The bombers proceeded to drop demolition, incendiary and anti-personnel bombs on the airfield and the quarters area before the fighters swooped down to strafe the airfield installations and grounded aeroplanes. Three P-40s and two P-43s were destroyed and 13 other P-40s sustained damage. Fortunately, only one person was injured.

A few P-40s were able to engage the raiders. Col Homer Sanders,

The shattered remains of the Ki-46 'Dinah' downed by the 26th's Lt Alvin Watson on 19 October 1942. The reconnaissance aircraft crashed in the jungle 40 miles south of Margherita, thus giving the 51st FG its first confirmed victory of the war. Note the distinctive 81st Sentai, 2nd Chutai marking on the aircraft's fin at the left of the photograph

51st FG commander, and his group engineering officer, Capt Charles Dunning, had just taken off for a reconnaissance mission when they spotted the incoming attackers. Climbing up behind the formation, the P-40 pilots attacked the 15 Ki-43 'Oscars' from the 50th and 64th Sentais that were flying as bomber escorts. Coming in on the right side of the formation, Sanders picked off the leader of the right element, but another 'Oscar' quickly chandelled onto Dunning's tail and shot him down. Sanders recorded that he continued to mix it up with the enemy for about 40 minutes until the 'Oscars' withdrew.

A flight of six P-40s had also taken off after the strafing had ended, chasing the raiders back into Burma. However, only Lt William R Rogers succeeded in making contact with the withdrawing force, downing an 'Oscar'. Col Sanders also received credit for two Ki-43s destroyed.

1Lt Ed Nollmeyer, who was destined to become the 26th's premier ace, scored his first victory 24 hours later when a formation of 'Oscars' strafed the satellite fields at Mohanbari and Mokelbari. Again giving chase to the

Members of the engineering section of the 26th FS's B Flight (the 'Eight Ball' detachment) pose alongside a suitably decorated P-40K at Mokelbari on 10 July 1943. The number '87' is barely visible on the Warhawk's fin on the original print. Seen standing, from left to right, are Sgt Hudson, S/Sgt Patchin, S/Sgt Washburn and T/Sgt Zietz. Kneeling, again from left to right, are S/Sgt Barclay, S/Sgt Maurer, S/Sgt Heiser, S/Sgt Schultz, Sgt Goddard and S/Sgt McCarron

A flight of Warhawks from the 26th FS operated from the satellite airfield at Mohanbari, in Assam, during 1942-43. Located on a British tea plantation, this building served as the pilots' alert shack throughout the war. The 26th FS was later replaced by a flight from the 80th FG

Japanese fighters as they headed for home, Nollmeyer used the superior straightline speed of his P-40 to hunt down a Ki-43 and destroy it about 20 miles south of Digboi. Earlier that same day, Lt Ira M Sussky (a 25th FS pilot attached to the 26th) had claimed a twin-engined reconnaissance aircraft near Dinjan to give his squadron its first confirmed victory.

The last Japanese attack against Dinjan came on 28 October, and this time the defenders were ready for them. Seven P-40s scrambled at 1240 hrs, and ten minutes later the first wave of 17 enemy bombers began attacking Mohanbari. One of the five P-40s to make contact in this initial interception was the aircraft flown by Lt K C 'Casey' Hynds, who later gave this vivid description of his first encounter with the enemy:

'I was on alert at Mohanbari. Sometime during the morning, one of the flight leaders and I took off for a two-hour patrol. Since the raids had started, we tried to keep two planes on patrol at 18,000 ft because our warning time for approaching enemy planes was so short. We had been on patrol for about 20 minutes when my leader experienced engine trouble and returned to base. About 15 minutes later, ops came on the radio: "All planes to maximum altitude. Enemy aircraft approaching very high".

'I had climbed to just over 20,000 ft, searching the sky above me for the enemy, when I heard on my radio: "Bombs falling on Chabua". I was directly over Chabua, and looking down I could see the explosions, but I could see no aircraft! Their camouflage paint was so good that they blended perfectly with the jungle below. Then they crossed the Brahmaputra – a river as wide as the Mississippi – and the nine-ship formation was very visible about 1500 ft below me. With full power, and all arming switches on, I started my dive. I was determined to get the lead bomber with my first pass. I asked ops if any fighters were reported with the bombers. "None reported", was the reply. I had news for them. There were six or eight fighters milling above the bombers.

'One fighter to my left pulled up as if to slip behind me when I passed, and he offered such as good target that I instinctively turned on him and opened fire. In my excitement, I had failed to turn on my gun sight, but the tracers flowing in front of his cowling only had to be moved to his engine and cockpit to effect the kill. Having previously only fired one gun at a time (and that a 0.30-cal in a P-39), I was absolutely overwhelmed by the damage that six 0.50-cals could do! I was practically on top of the Jap, and those guns just ate up that plane. He was later found, crashed on the west bank of the Brahmaputra.

'The pass at the fighter had spoiled my run on the bombers, and with so many of his friends around, I knew I had to get some distance and then some altitude before trying it again. By the time I had enough of both, I couldn't see them – but I did see a lone P-40, and eased over to join him. We hadn't been together two minutes when I saw a formation of bombers heading east toward the Naga Hills, and to wherever in Burma they had come from. I notified my friend and turned east. My communication must not have been understood, because he turned west. The bombers were about eight miles away and about 500 ft below my altitude. With full throttle, I could see that I would catch them, but oh so slowly.

'Prior to getting within range, I was surrounded by puffs of black smoke from anti-aircraft fire. I had seen no AA burst near the bomber formation, and wondered why the British AA unit below had become so intent on a lone fighter when they had ignored the large bomber formation. Curiously, I didn't worry about the danger, since it was "friendly fire"!

'As I got within firing range, I was directly behind the right rear plane in the nine-ship formation. My tracers were going beneath his right wing, but with a slight correction I brought them up to the right engine, which burst into flame almost immediately. Firing my guns continuously, I made a slow left turn. Sweeping the tracers through the entire formation. The guns quit firing just before the last aircraft passed through my gun sight. Continuing the turn, I went into a slow dive toward Mohanbari. Out of ammo, and after having been on patrol before the raid and racing at full throttle for much of the time since then, I was damned low on fuel.

'I glanced back at the Japanese formation. One plane was about a mile behind the others (so far away I couldn't count them), and I thought the SOB had put that fire out. Ops came on the air with, "Mohanbari has bomb damage to the runway. Do not land there. Go to (Sadiya)". I didn't know the field, didn't know where to look for it, and knowing I didn't have enough fuel to fool around, continued on to Mohanbari. I had only to bounce over one crater and guide around another on my landing roll to get safely "home".'

K C Hynds was credited with two confirmed victories for the mission. Further claims for one probable and six damaged were awarded to four other pilots. Hynds had spent eight months in Panama flying P-39s prior to being assigned to the CBI, and in November 1942 he ferried a new P-40K to China. While there, he was transferred to the 23rd FG's 75th FS, and he spent the rest of his combat tour in China but scored no further victories.

Japanese aircraft did not return to Assam during 1942. The two squadrons of the 51st FG remained on alert, however, continuing to patrol the Hump, but they also began to branch out with offensive operations against ground targets in northern Burma. Throughout the winter of 1942-43, the P-40s bombed and strafed bridges, roads, trains and the enemy airfields at Myitkyina and Lashio. On occasion, they even dropped leaflets and gifts on Burmese villages behind Japanese lines in an attempt to boost the morale of the residents.

P-40 units in Assam were under constant threat from the air, so groundcrews made a great effort to camouflage their fighters with whatever foliage they could find. Here, a Warhawk has been covered with branches in its jungle revetment. Note also the bamboo matting on which the fighter is parked

NEW YEAR, — NEW CHALLENGES —

As 1943 began, the 25th and 26th FSs began to note signs of renewed activity by the Japanese. Although British ground forces under Brigadier Orde Wingate had commenced guerrilla operations behind enemy lines in northern Burma, the Japanese army had begun to push from Mandalay toward Fort Hertz, in northernmost Burma. The latter site was a key communications outpost that also boasted an emergency airfield, and to lose it would have

1Lt John F 'Jake' Coonan of the 26th FS scored one confirmed victory and one damaged flying this P-40K on 25 February 1943. The 51st FG was involved in a large air battle on this day, its pilots claiming 12 Japanese aircraft confirmed destroyed, 14 probables and six damaged, all for no loss

Capt Charles 'Hank' Colwell and his crewchief pose in front of their P-40K, 'White 82'. This 26th FS Warhawk is painted in standard two-colour camouflage, and displays US ARMY titling on the undersurfaces of its wings. Beneath the fighter's windshield is Colwell's name and two victory flags, although the pilot's official score was one confirmed and one damaged. Colwell was killed in a flying accident on 2 June 1943

been a serious blow to Hump operations. Responding to the Japanese push, the 51st FG threw itself into action in support of the Allied effort to sever the enemy's vital lines of communication and supply.

Accordingly, the Assam airfields once again began to feature high on the target list for the Japanese Army Air Force. 'Red Alert' air raid warnings sounded at the strips surrounding Dinjan on 10 January and 11 February, but on neither occasion did Japanese formations actually attack. Then late in the afternoon of 23 February, the 98th Sentai hit Chabua with 27 bombers. Dropping down out of a cloudy sky, the attackers unloaded about 50 bombs onto the field and then escaped back into the overcast before the defending fighters of the 51st FG could make contact. And although the raid had caused little damage, it was just a warm-up.

The 51st FG operated a string of observation posts in the Naga Hills, east of the Dinjan bases, to provide air raid warnings in much the same way as Gen Chennault's warning net did in China. At 0635 hrs on 25 February, post KC-8 at Khola Ga radioed a report of a large enemy formation approaching from Burma. Within minutes, 32 P-40s of the 25th and 26th FSs were clawing for altitude. The Japanese force, which consisted of 27 bombers and 21 fighters, had flown north from their base at Shwebo, in Burma, but had been hampered by clouds near the target area. The aircraft overflew Sookerating, then turned 180 degrees and descended below the cloud to make their bombing run. This manoeuvre gave the P-40 pilots the chance they needed to effect an interception.

Capt Kuroe of the 64th Sentai, who was leading the high flight of 'Oscar' escorts, reported seeing one P-40 dive on the bombers as other appeared above him. One bomber exploded, and then more Warhawks began to attack. Maj Akera, leading the 64th Sentai, evaded two P-40s attacking from above, only to come face-to-face with two more in a head-on duel. He lost, and the Ki-43 spun into the ground on fire, carrying the veteran pilot to his death. Akera had been made CO of the 64th just three days before.

The P-40s pressed home their attack between Sookerating and Digboi as the Japanese withdrew. The 'Oscars' proved unable to provide cover for the bombers, and as a result the 51st FG experienced its most successful day of combat over Assam. All the P-40s landed safely, and the combined score of the pilots was 12 confirmed, 14 probables and six damaged. In the 25th FS, victories were credited to Capt Earl Livesay and 1Lts Jack Irwin and Ira

Sussky, whilst the 26th FS's scorers were Capts Charles Colwell and 'Swede' Svenningson, and 1Lts Lyle Boley, Jake Coonan, John Fouts Jr, Arthur Gregg, Ed Nollmeyer, William Packard and Alvin Watson.

BIGGER BOMBS

John E Barr, the pilot who had led the P-40s off the USS *Ranger* in May 1942, was an ideas man. Now serving as executive officer of the 51st FG, Col Barr was on the field at Dinjan one day in early 1943 when he saw a pile of 1000-lb demolition bombs that had been delivered for use by a B-25 unit that shared the base with the P-40s. He looked at the bombs, and he looked at a Warhawk parked nearby. The 51st FG had been dropping 300- and 500-lb bombs on a regular basis with deadly accuracy. A P-40 ought to be able to do the same thing with a 'thousand-pounder' Barr figured. So, he called a group of pilots together and began to test his theory. One of those men was 1Lt Hazen Helvey, who recounted the experience many years later;

'The 1000-lb bomb activity was very personal to me. "Big Ed" Nollmeyer and I were from the 26th, Lts (John) Keith, (Robert) McClung and (William) Bertram were from the 25th, and Col Barr was from headquarters. All were hand-picked fighter pilots, and I'm sure none had any reservations about the skill, courage, resoluteness and dedication of his associates in the execution of the bombing missions, as well as in their respect for each other.

'Flying the bomb off the ground was the simple part. The targets assigned for destruction by this group were specific, difficult to hit and well protected. A near miss was worthless, especially when dive-bombing railroad bridges and key buildings, or skip-bombing tunnels. Delay fuses were used in skip-bombing, but all bridges required instantaneous fuses. The key was to get as close as you could without getting involved in the explosion. In several instances, pilots' concentration on their target was so intense that they flew low enough for their planes to be damaged from their own bomb blast.

'We tried to dive at about a 60-degree angle, and the speed of the P-40 was usually between 350 and 400 mph. You never saw the instant results of your dive, as you were too busy taking evasive action, and also too blacked out from pulling out of the dive. However, you could hear the exclamations of your comrades – or the lack of exclamations (if you missed the target)! We did not have bombsights – just the regular gunsight. You just placed the vertical line of the gunsight onto the target and flew exactly down that path. Your degree of success depended upon how well you did just that.'

The first recorded use of 'thousand-pounders' on a live target came on 21 March 1943 when Col Barr and his five pilots attacked Moguang, in Burma, protected by a further two P-40s flying top cover. All six bombs were reported to have hit in the target area, and the aeroplanes returned safely to base. In the months that followed, Col Barr trained nearly all of the 51st FG pilots in his techniques for dropping 1000-lb bombs.

FINAL ENCOUNTER

The 51st FG encountered the Japanese just once more in the air over Assam and Burma. On 8 April 1943, 1Lt Charles T Streit of the 26th FS took off in the squadron's stripped-down P-40E-1 'No 72' to intercept a Ki-46 'Dinah' 'Photo Joe' that was scouting the Assam bases. Forty years later, Charlie Streit gave this description of his aeroplane;

'The exterior paint job was Olive Drab, and it had no unusual markings. Here's how it was stripped down: all armour plate was removed; all radios removed except for one; four of the six 0.50-calibre machine guns removed, leaving only one in each wing; and only half a load of ammo was left in the wing boxes for each gun. The fuel tanks were left intact, but only half a load of fuel was put in. I can't say how much lighter the plane was, but it flew a lot better, and could climb at twice the rate of a normal P-40.'

Lt Streit filed the following report immediately after returning from shooting down the Ki-46;

'At 1156 hrs I was airborne in "No 72", our cut-down P-40E-1. I circled the field twice, climbing at 1700 ft per minute. As I reached 8500 ft, I was called by control and they gave the position of the target as overhead at 15,000 ft. I increased rpm to 2700 and manifold pressure to 38 inches hg. I then climbed at 2000 ft per minute. Control gave the direction of the target as south. I immediately headed in that direction. They then immediately called again and gave the target's direction as north-west.

'I turned to that heading, and looking up in a cloud bank, located the enemy plane cruising 1000 ft above me and a quarter-mile away. I took a heading to cut him off. He perceived that I was doing so and gaining on him, so he levelled off, and banking slightly to the right and nosing down, took a north-east heading and tried to reach a cloud bank. His acceleration was greater than mine, and he drew away rapidly. I fire-walled the throttle and RPM, and took an east-northeast heading to cut him off. My indicated airspeed was 270 at that time. I gained slowly, and by the time I reached an indicated airspeed of 320, I was directly behind him. We were at an altitude of 8000 ft. He continued to descend, and I pulled up to him rapidly.

'I turned on my gun switches and gunsight, and waiting until I was at point-blank range, aimed at his right engine nacelle and pulled the trigger. I observed the tracers going into his right engine nacelle, and then my guns stopped firing. I pulled up and over his right wing and noticed black smoke. I kept ahead and parallel of him and charged my guns. Then I made a deflection pass using a "Lazy 8" pattern. I repeated this four times before my right gun fired. I made two more passes in this manner and concentrated on his left motor. His right engine was still running, but smoking more and more.

'The observer was facing rearward and kept following me with his head. The only evasive action the pilot was using was a slight turn now and then, which was very ineffective. He did not return my fire. I noticed that we were reaching the mountains, and trying to keep him away from the mountainous area, I slid over him to make a pass from that direction. As I slid over him I noticed one of the wings smouldering and some smoke emanating from a point to the rear of the nacelle. I started my dive from an advantage of 500 ft and 300 yards distance. He banked away from me and turned toward the valley to evade my pass. Just as I was about to fire from 100 yards, his right wing caught on fire. I pulled away to the left and above him at an altitude of 5000 ft and watched. His plane snapped over in a roll to the right, and pointing its nose at the ground, he dove in.

'He was almost entirely enveloped in flame by the time he hit the ground, and then he exploded. I circled and tried to give my position, but after following him down to the ground I could not give the co-ordinates. I climbed higher, and after a few attempts gave an approximate position. Four P-40s were despatched to find my position. They finally located me and observed the scene of the crash when I led them to it. They confirmed the position, and I returned to base at 1305.'

Streit's victory was the last victory attributed to the 51st whilst it was assigned to the Tenth Air Force. The group continued to fly from its Assam bases throughout the summer of 1943, although the monsoon season hampered operations for much of that time. Then, on 12 September 1943, orders arrived from Tenth Air Force headquarters – the 51st FG was to move to China, where it would join Gen Chennault's ever-growing Fourteenth Air Force.

THE 'BURMA BANSHEES'

After nearly a year of training on the new Republic P-47 Thunderbolt, the eager pilots of the 80th FG figured they were on their way to England to fight the Luftwaffe when they shipped out of New York harbour on 10 May 1943. But the convoy didn't head east across the Atlantic. Instead it went south to Cape Town, South Africa, and then up the east coast of Africa and on to Karachi, arriving on 29 June.

A 15-mile truck ride took the unit to the New Malir Cantonment on the edge of the Sind Desert, where the men found no P-47s waiting for them, but instead just a few war-weary Curtiss Hawk 81s (which they called P-40Bs) that had been retired from combat after duty in China with both the AVG and the 23rd FG. Training duly commenced on these aeroplanes, and within a few weeks new P-40N-1s began to arrive for assignment to the 88th, 89th, and 90th FSs. The next surprise came when a cadre of experienced pilots from the 51st FG were transferred in to the 80th FG to replace a number of officers in key leadership positions.

With the 51st FG moving up to China, the Tenth Air Force wanted to retain a core of experienced fighter pilots in the new group taking over in Assam. Therefore, command of the 80th passed from Maj Albert Evans, who had trained the group in the USA, to Col Ivan McElroy. Evans instead became executive officer, before reassuming command in 1944 when McElroy completed his overseas tour. Another combat veteran to transfer in was Capt John 'Swede' Svenningson from the 26th FS, who became CO of the 89th FS.

Coincidentally, the first squadron to deploy to Assam was the 89th FS, which established itself on the strips at Nagaghuli and Sadiya in early September 1943. The 88th FS followed later in the month, settling at Mokelbari and Lilibari. Once again a substantial swap of personnel took place as 12 pilots of the 89th FS

Technicians work on a 25th FS P-40E at Sadiya, in India, where a flight of Warhawks operated off of a golf course fairway! Armourer Art Sitas poses in front of the fighter, and behind him, perched on the wing, is a Curtiss-Wright 'tech rep'. Note the primitive outdoor setting, which was typical of conditions in Assam

transferred to the 51st FG, and 16 pilots from the 25th FS were in turn reassigned to the 89th FS.

Although monsoon weather subsequently hampered operations for both the 88th and 89th FSs throughout the autumn of 1943, both units were able to fly enough sorties to become familiar with the territory, and the mission. Their assignment was essentially the same as that carried out by the 51st FG during the previous year – defend the Hump bases, and fly offensive missions against ground targets in Burma. The 80th FG's final unit, the 90th FS was based at Jorhat, out of range of targets in Burma, until March 1944.

It was during the group's first months in-theatre that 89th FS pilot Lt Freeling 'Dixie' Clower came up with the design for the distinctive white skull nose markings that the 80th would adopt for all of its P-40s. The flying skull design gave rise to the group's nickname, the 'Burma Banshees'.

The 80th FG's first encounter with the enemy occurred on 10 December 1943, and Capt William S Harrell, a flight commander in the 89th FS at that time, gave the following description of the fight which ensued;

'I was leading a flight of four P-40s patrolling the Hump route in the vicinity of Fort Hertz in northern Burma. We were flying at approximately 25,000 ft when we sighted a Japanese formation of three bombers (Ki-21 'Sallys') escorted by four fighters ('Oscars'). The formation was headed north toward Fort Hertz. We attacked immediately, and the enemy jettisoned their bombs and external tanks, turning south toward Myitkyina airfield. One of the escort fighters turned into me head-on, hitting my engine and causing an oil leak. I shot this fighter down with a short burst, seeing him roll over, smoking, and plunge into the ground.

'I proceeded to press the attack on one of the bombers, flying on the left wing. I saw hits in both engines, with flames coming from each, and the bomber fell out of formation, rolled over on fire, and headed toward the ground. As I pulled up from the attack, I saw that my wingman, Lt (Robert) McCarty, was still with me, and that Lt (George) Whitley, the Number 3 man in the flight, was pressing home an attack against the bomber on the right wing of the three-ship formation. Lt Whitley shot this bomber down. Lt (Dodd) Shepard, Number 4 man in our flight, also shot a fighter down on this pass.

'That left one bomber and two fighters in the Japanese formation. Seeing the remaining bomber head south, I attacked. I shot him in the wing roots and his engines, but I couldn't get him to go down or to catch fire. I stayed on the attack too long and damned near flew into him, pushing the stick forward and going under him too closely. As I came out in front of the bomber, the nose gunner had a very close shot at my aircraft, and he made good use of it – he filled my plane full of holes. I had loosened my shoulder straps so I could lean forward to be closer to the gunsight and to

1Lt Donald W Maxwell of the 25th FS is seen with his *LIZ* (P-40K-1 42-46261) in a bamboo grove at Sadiya in 1943. The fighter sports the 25th FS's distinctive 'Assam Draggins' dragonsmouth marking, which boasted blue or black lips and a red tongue. Maxwell transferred to the 80th FG in July 1943

89th FS Flight Leader Capt William S Harrell scored two aerial victories in his squadron's first encounter with Japanese aircraft on 10 December 1943. Harrell's P-40N-1 displays the distinctive skull marking of the 80th FG. Applied without the use of templates, each skull was different. Here, red 'blood' flows from the jaws of Harrell's marking

clear my tail better. This action saved my life, for a bullet struck the left side of the canopy, went behind my back, and exited the right side. Lt McCarty shot this bomber down.

'I pulled up, checked out my aircraft, and it seemed to be running okay, although it was losing a good bit of oil. I was alone now, having been separated from my wingman when he finished off the last bomber. I headed south, hoping to pick up the enemy fighters still in the area. And I did. An "Oscar" and I saw each other at the same time and turned into each other for a head-on pass. I started firing and saw hits on his aircraft. He rolled onto his back and seemed to be out of control as he went through a broken cloud layer. I did not see him hit the ground, nor did I observe smoke or fire from his aircraft – consequently, I did not claim a victory following this engagement.

'My guns stopped firing on the last pass, and I thought they had jammed. We discovered later, however, that I was out of ammunition. I was losing oil badly and decided to land at Fort Hertz rather than try flying back over the mountains to my home base at Sadiya. I proceeded back to Fort Hertz, had my wheels down and was turning on base leg when I saw a C-46 attempting a belly landing with an "Oscar" shooting him up badly. The "Oscar" must have seen me, because he pulled up and headed south without beating up the airfield.

'I pulled my wheels up and headed back over the mountains to Sadiya. Once I was through the pass, at 5240 ft, the flight was all "downhill". I followed a riverbed, planning to belly in on a sandbar if the engine quit. I was pretty low by now and could see herds of water buffalo drinking in the river – didn't want to land on of those herds, as the buffs were pretty tough characters! But the engine never missed a beat; I reached Sadiya and landed safely but badly, as oil on the front windscreen obscured my vision.'

Bill Harrell was soon promoted to command the 89th FS, and he went on to fly 158 combat missions (totalling 450 flying hours) during his tour. As was typical in the 80th FG, he had no further opportunities for air-to-air-combat. Harrell made a career for himself in the military, and retired from the post-war USAF with the rank of major general.

The total score for 10 December was five destroyed and two damaged by the 89th FS, and one probable and two damaged by the 88th FS, which engaged the 'Oscars' attacking Fort Hertz.

SOLO ATTACK

Three days later, a much larger enemy formation flew up from Burma to attack the Hump bases at Dinjan. Again, both the 88th and 89th FSs got in on the action, and a total of five 'Oscars' and one 'Sally' were credited as destroyed. At the beginning of the fight, however, only one P-40 was in position to face the Japanese formation of 24 'Sally' bombers and 35 'Oscar' fighters. That P-40 was flown by 2Lt Phil

2Lt Phil Adair's first *Lulu Belle* was P-40N-1 42-104550, and as this photograph shows, it boasted whitewalled tyres on the main gear and tailwheel! The marking on the hubcaps is a flying buzzard holding a bomb in its talons. Like all P-40N-1s in the 80th FG, Adair's aeroplane carried six wing guns, which was unusual for this model of Warhawk (factory-built with just four 0.50-cal guns), and may have been a field modification

Adair of the 89th FS, who never forgot the experience. He had flown an early morning patrol mission and was back at Nagaghuli when the red alert was sounded. Sgt Carol Peake, his crewchief, had just finished servicing their P-40N-1, *Lulu Belle*, so Adair took off immediately. This is his account of the mission;

'We had a standing SOP that on red alert, we would all scramble and rendezvous over the field at 20,000 ft, maintaining radio silence to avoid warning possible intruders. After becoming airborne, I buckled up and started climbing over the field, watching for the other flight members to get off and join up. By the time I reached 12,000 ft over the field, none were off yet, but I could see what looked like a flight of four aircraft in the distance, but couldn't identify them. However, on my next circuit it became apparent that what I was seeing was not a flight of four, but something considerably larger.

'At this point I called Control and asked if there were any friends in the area. Control came back with a negative, but said they had reports of unknowns about 40 miles to the east. I responded back that the unknowns were much closer – 15 miles or so east of the base complex, and appeared to be on a north-west heading, giving the grid location. I then informed control that I was leaving the rendezvous point to investigate, as none of my flight was airborne yet, and no friendlies were in the area.

'Shortly after leaving my spot above the field, and getting much closer to the unknowns, I could see that instead of four aircraft there were four flights. I kept climbing and took up a course to bring me behind and above the formation. It seemed like they were headed north of the base complex, so they could make a 180 and line up their bomb run so they would be outbound after they had dropped their bombs. I so informed Control and was really angry when they came back with a "Negative-Negative", for they had reliable reports from ground stations that the unknowns were far to the east. As far as I could tell, any fighters we had airborne were being sent there.

'By this time I was at about 18,000 ft, and above the bombers, closing from behind so I could monitor their progress. Watching the bombers, and with the haze that cut visibility, I had not seen the Japanese fighters yet. But soon I discovered they were all over the place, flying individually instead of in pairs or other arrangements. I had climbed up almost to the middle of the trailing fighters, and they had not seen me. I figured that if I kept

2Lt Adair single-handedly attacked a large Japanese formation on 13 December 1943 near Chabua, claiming one aircraft destroyed and three damaged. He also shot down two 'Oscars' on 17 May 1944. He is seen here with his second *Lulu Belle*, which had a red propeller spinner to denote its assignment to the 89th FS

my course, I would soon be on top of everything, which I did. When they rolled out of their turn and took up a course, it was clear that I had guessed right about their intentions. I called Control and gave them the bad news, and an ETA for the enemy force, and I asked if our fighters were near enough to help. I got a negative on that also, so there I sat, on top by myself. I had a decision to make, and it was one I didn't particularly like to think about. I simply could not sit up there with a bird's eye view and watch the Japanese bomb the primary target complex for our area, and my home base, without doing everything possible to prevent it.

'I carefully positioned myself above the fighters and the bomber formation so I could hit the bombers just before I thought they would reach their bomb release point. I decided on an attack from high above on the left, trying to get some shots down into the lead flight at maximum range, dropping back to the left echelon flight and then swinging around behind to shoot at the third and fourth flights on the right echelon. This was a pretty wild scheme, and I knew there wasn't much chance of doing any real damage, but I hoped to get enough tracers across their bow to mess things up enough to affect their bombing accuracy.

'It worked out pretty well. I could see some bouncing around in the formation, but things went so quickly that I was behind the last flight without being able to see what damage, if any, I was doing. I concentrated on the last bomber in the fourth flight, zeroing in on his left engine, and I saw some flashes as my overtake speed caused me to go under and past him. I saw a break to the right, but as soon as I cleared the bombers I saw several Zeros coming at me. I immediately went into my planned escape manoeuvre, which was stick full forward in the left corner into a negative-G outside roll, then into a high-speed dive. I stayed in the dive until I figured I had gone far enough to shake the fighters, pulled out and looked around and saw I was by myself. The Zeros were going back to the bomber formation.

'As soon as I could see that I was not being followed, I climbed back on top and behind the formation again. I don't know if they didn't see me in the haze, but nobody made a move to cut me off, so I started another pass on the bombers. But before I could get near them, it looked like every Zero in the sky was turning into me. It was obvious I wasn't going to get a shot at the bombers, but there were plenty of Zeros, and with a good speed advantage from my dive, I just went through them, taking deflection shots at whatever I could get my sights on. I could see that I was getting some good hits in, and the engine of one of the Zeros I hit looked like it was on fire. But being by myself, I could not afford to dwell on the ones I was shooting at, so I concentrated on what was in front of me, not what was behind, believing my overtake speed would get me out of range.

'After going through my escape manoeuvre again, I climbed back on top. It seemed like a good time to try for a Zero. Picking the one at the top rear, I started a pass. But he knew I was there and turned so there was no possibility of my hitting him. So I just picked the next one. He started a turn also, but not before I could get a shot at him. His gear started to drop – pulling back on the throttle and getting firmly behind him, I could see that he seemed to lose control and fell off into a spiral dive. I followed him down, moving off to one side to watch, and saw him crash into the jungle in the Naga Hills.'

Adair made one more climb back toward the retreating enemy formation, but this time the 'Oscars' boxed him in and shot up his P-40. He escaped once more in a power dive, and this time he pointed *Lulu Belle* toward home, about 125 miles away. The damaged fighter flew extremely nose-heavy, so Adair took to flying it inverted for minutes at a time so that he could rest his arms. When the engine loaded up he would roll back right side up and let it clear, then roll inverted again;

'I don't know how many times we flipped, but eventually I found myself about a half-mile from Nagaghuli at an altitude of about 1000 ft. Turning to approach the runway straight in from the south, and inverted, I came back on the power to bring me down to the runway, and at the last possible moment I flipped the gear handle down and squeezed the pump switch. When I saw down and locked, I rolled *Lulu Belle* over, hit the flap switch, and cut the throttle. The landing wasn't the usual three-pointer and was in the wrong direction, but I couldn't have cared less. We were down, and in one piece.'

Phil Adair was credited with one 'Oscar' destroyed, plus one 'Sally' and two 'Oscars' damaged, in the fight – the mission also earned him a Silver Star for bravery. The rest of his flight eventually got airborne, but only 2Lt James May was able to attack the enemy formation. He destroyed one bomber, but return fire knocked out his engine and he was forced to bail out. May suffered burns, but was able to return to service in the 89th FS.

Meanwhile, the 88th FS was also able to get into the action on 13 December, apparently running into the same formation that had been previously attacked by the 89th. Capts Patrick Randall and George Hamilton were each credited with a half-victory for the 'Oscar' they shot down, while other Ki-43 kills were credited to 88th FS pilots Capt Owen Allred, 1Lt Ralph Anderson and 2Lt Brooks Emerick.

The 80th FG's last aerial action of 1943 was an all-89th FS show. A flight of P-40s was dive-bombing at Myitkyina on 28 December when four 'Oscars' attacked the last element. One P-40 was damaged, but 1Lt Freeling Clower and 2Lt Charlie Hardy each claimed a Ki-43. The unit was back in action over Fort Hertz on 18 January 1944, claiming one 'Oscar' destroyed by 2Lt Fred Evans and three damaged for no loss.

THE 80TH'S BEST DAY

The first months of 1944 brought a high level of activity for the 80th FG, as the unit was heavily engaged in the support of an advance by US ground forces into northern Burma. The ground troops, commanded by Maj Gen Frank Merrill, were tasked with breaking through the Japanese frontline at Ledo, in Assam, and heading on to Myitkyina, in Burma, in order to create a land link with China. The success of the offensive depended on how quickly 'Merrill's Marauders' could neutralise the Japanese presence in the jungle areas of Assam, and the 80th FG was called on to serve as 'flying artillery' in support of this effort.

Armourers of the 89th FS tow a load of 1000-lb bombs out to the flightline at Nagaghuli, where squadron Warhawks await their deadly cargoes. The first aeroplane in line ('White 62') was the P-40N-5 assigned to Lt Dodd V Shepard. Most of the sorties flown by the 80th FG during 1944 saw the P-40s performing ground attack missions in support of 'Merrill's Marauders'

Despite Japanese aircraft now being rarely encountered, on 27 March the 80th FG recorded its biggest aerial victory of the war. The day not only saw eight pilots of the 89th and 90th FSs score 18 confirmed victories between them, but it also witnessed the first kills for a young flight officer by the name of Samuel E 'Gene' Hammer, who claimed two Ki-21s. Flying with the 90th FS, he would subsequently become the 80th FG's only single-engined fighter ace of the war – the 80th FG also provided administrative control for the P-38-equipped 459th FS, which produced six aces (see *Osprey Aircraft of the Aces 14 - P-38 Lightning Aces of the Pacific and CBI* for further details).

Going one better than Hammer's double score, 2Lt Herbert 'Hal' Doughty's trio of kills, and a damaged, was the highest single-mission tally recorded by any 80th FG pilot. More than 50 years later, he penned this account of his only encounter with enemy aircraft;

'I arrived in India in December 1943 and joined the 80th in early 1944 in upper Assam. I was assigned to the outpost at Sadiya, where A Flight of the 89th FS was stationed. We had six P-40Ns, 12 pilots and support crews. Our main job was Hump patrol and air defence alert. Once in a

On 27 March 1944 Warhawk flights from the 89th and 90th FSs attacked a Japanese formation near Ledo, Assam, and destroyed 18 aircraft without loss. The pilots involved were, from left to right, 1Lt Ralph Ward, 2Lt Gale Lyon, 2Lt Joe Patton and Flt Off S E 'Gene' Hammer of the 90th FS, all of whom got two victories apiece, and the 89th's 1Lt R D Bell (three victories) and 2Lts Percy Marshall (two victories), Ray McReynold (two victories) and Hal Doughty (three victories)

Crewchief Curt Grant (left) and pilot Hal Doughty of the 89th FS pose next to their P-40N-1, 'White 55', at Sadiya in the spring of 1944. The scoreboard shows three full victory flags for confirmed kills and a half flag for one damaged, all of which were scored by Doughty on 27 March 1944. He once took Grant up for a ride in this aeroplane, letting the crewchief control the fighter and fire the guns as he sat on the pilot's lap!

while we would get a bomb and go after a target in Burma. Sadiya was a really enjoyable place to be. We kept a five-man hunting party out and did pretty well in the fresh meat department. Mail and visitors, or replacements, usually arrived in the PT-17, with baggage tied to the lower wing. Our quarters there were very good – British outpost administrative facilities.

'27 March 1944 was a big day. Four of us were on alert. 1Lt R D Bell was flight leader, and his wingman was Lt Percy Marshall – element lead was Lt Ray McReynolds,

and I was his wingman. The scramble signal (three shots from a 0.45-cal pistol) sounded, so we cranked up and got airborne. No warm-ups or mag checks on a scramble! Fighter control gave us a vector and reported many targets at Angels 20 – up where the P-40 got really sick.

'We climbed through two or three layers of rather thin clouds, and as we broke out on top at 20,000 ft the Jap formation was just rolling out of a right turn. At least 18 "Helen" bombers and a swarm of Zeros. R D called "Tally Ho" and said, "A Flight, arm your guns". I suggested we drop our belly tanks, and he agreed. My engine quit immediately, as I hadn't switched to my internal tanks! It caught right away, and by this time we were right on the formation.

'On the first pass through I could see two bombers burning besides the one I got. By the time we got back in from the other side there were several smoke columns along their path, and the Zeros were into it. Percy Marshall was shot down, landed in friendly territory and was back with us that afternoon.'

In addition to Doughty's three victories (two 'Oscars' and a 'Helen'), Bell got two fighters and a bomber, and Marshall and McReynolds each claimed one fighter and one bomber. A flight of four P-40s from the 90th FS, led by 1Lt Ralph Ward, was also in the area, and they joined the scrap. The unit had moved up to Moran that month to adds its weight to the Burma campaign, and this was the first of only two missions throughout the entire war in which its pilots filed claims for enemy aircraft.

Three pilots from the 89th FS pose in front of 1Lt R D Bell's Warhawk at Nagaghuli in April or May 1944. They are, from left to right, 1Lt Ralph 'Dusty' Rhodes and 2Lts George Seifert and Joel Martinez – the latter pilot would be posted Missing in Action on 16 June 1944. Bell's 'White 52' (P-40N-1 42-105234) displays three victory flags, which means that this photograph was taken after the interception of 27 March 1944

Blue-nosed P-40N-1 'White 71, nicknamed *Ruth Marie*, was the regular aircraft of Flt Off Gene Hammer of the 90th FS during the spring and summer of 1944. It displays the two victory flags he earned in the 27 March 1944 air battle, although records show Hammer was flying 'White 89' on that day. He scored three more victories on 14 December 1944 in a P-47D to become the 80th FG's sole single-engined ace of the war

Ward's wingman on the mission was 2Lt Gale Lyon, his element leader was 2Lt Joe Patton, and the last pilot in the flight was 'Gene' Hammer, who had only recently joined the squadron. The four pilots had a field day, scoring two kills apiece as they chased the Japanese formation back into Burma. Ward was shooting up a third 'Helen' bomber at low altitude when an 'Oscar' made a pass at him and hit his P-40 in several places. The P-40 pilot ran out of ammunition at this point, so he called it a day and headed for home.

As previously mentioned, 'Gene' Hammer would later 'make ace' when on 14 December 1944 he destroyed three Ki-44 'Tojos' in a scrap south of Bhamo, bringing his score to exactly five. By then the 90th FS had long since traded in its P-40s for P-47Ds (see *Osprey Aircraft of the Aces 26 - Mustang and Thunderbolt Aces of the Pacific and CBI* for further details). Sadly, Hammer was killed in a traffic accident in Texas in 1953.

One by one, the Warhawk squadrons converted to P-47s during the summer of 1944. The last kills credited to 80th FG P-40s were claimed by the 88th FS on 9 July 1944, and one of the pilots on that mission was 1Lt Robert Gale. By then the 88th FS had become the first squadron to move into Burma, operating from the jungle airbase at Shingbwiyang. The following account is Gale's recollection of the mission;

'Four of us took off on a bombing mission. It was overcast and we climbed up through it. When we broke out of the clouds Capt Owen Allred (the flight leader) said, "There's bandits up there. Arm your bombs and drop them". I looked up and saw several Zeros (I learned later there were about 30 of them). Of course, climbing with the bomb load – two "250-pounders" – our speed was very low. We could do nothing but dive for cover.

'In the enemy attack, my aeroplane sustained several hits in the tail section. My wingman, Lt Tom O'Connor, was shot down. He bailed out (we later saw his 'chute) and according to intelligence he was captured, tortured and killed. The rest of the flight was scattered after that initial attack. I darted in and out of the clouds until I came upon an unsuspecting victim, slipped in behind him, and got off a good burst. When I last saw him, his canopy had blown off, he was in flames and he was headed for the ground.

'My second Zero kill was much like the first, except that I was only able to get in a short burst. I could see that I had hit him on the left wing, but I didn't think I hit the cockpit. However, he flipped over on his back and did a Split-S. He was only between 500 and 700 ft above the ground, and I was sure that he couldn't pull out in time. I got credit for the first Zero that day. Several pilots spotted the wreckage of the second one the next day and gave me credit for that one, too. All of this action took place within a few miles of the field.'

Capt Allred was credited with one destroyed, one probable and two damaged, whilst his remaining wingmen, 2Lt Calvin Baldwin and Lt O'Connor, were each credited with one fighter destroyed.

These victories raised the 80th FG's tally of enemy aircraft destroyed to 40 while operating the Curtiss fighter. Within weeks of this action taking place, the Warhawks had begun to be replaced by Thunderbolts, although by then the venerable P-40 had well and truly left its mark in the skies over Assam and northern Burma.

1Lt Bob Gale (right) of the 88th FS enjoys a reunion with his brother, Sgt Don Gale, of the 375th Infantry Division at Myitkyina, in Burma. 1Lt Gale was among the first pilots of the 88th FS to fly into the small airstrip at Myitkyina on 3 July 1944 to commence operations against Japanese ground forces holding the city. The P-40N behind them appears to have been transferred in from the 89th FS

CHINA BUILD-UP

The 23rd FG began its second year of combat operations with the war situation in China little changed from July 1942. The Japanese still had them surrounded on three sides, with significant strongholds in the Hankow area and on the China coast, plus occupation forces in Indo-China, Thailand and Burma. The 23rd FG (along with the handful of other units that made up Gen Chennault's Fourteenth Air Force) continued to operate from its 650-mile string of airfields from Yunnanyi to Hengyang, and all supplies for the group still had to be flown in over the Hump.

However, 12 months of combat had transformed the four squadrons of the 23rd FG. No longer were war-weary AVG veterans and 'green' AAF

pilots expected to hold the line against the enemy. The 'Flying Tigers' had long since left for home, and the Army pilots had transformed the group into a hard-hitting, highly effective combat unit.

Their combat record for that first year proved the point. As of 4 July 1943, pilots of the 23rd FG had been credited with 171 confirmed victories for the cost of 15 pilots killed in aerial combat and nine men killed on the ground by Japanese bombing and strafing. Of the 15 pilots lost, eight had been brought down by ground

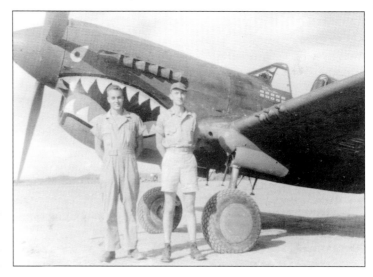

Col Bruce K Holloway (right) and crewchief Sgt Fred Lonneman pose in China with their P-40K in late July or early August 1943. At that stage the 23rd FG commander's score stood at ten confirmed. Holloway claimed three more kills in late August to raise his final tally to 13 destroyed, creating a three-way tie for the title of the highest scoring American P-40 pilot

Maj-Gen Claire Chennault, centre, poses proudly at Kunming with his two top fighter leaders (both aces) in the summer of 1943. Col Clinton D 'Casey' Vincent (left) commanded the Fourteenth Air Force's Forward Echelon and Lt Col Bruce Holloway led the 23rd FG

Col Clinton D 'Casey' Vincent flies his P-40K *Peggy II* over Kunming Lake in 1943. As commanding officer of the Forward Echelon, and later the 68th Composite Wing, Vincent scored six victories over China before Gen Chennault restricted him from further combat flying in late 1943. Note the AVG tiger decal on the fuselage. This aeroplane was named after Vincent's wife

fire. At the same time, four aces (Holloway, Goss, Little and DuBois) had been created, and they remained on flying status with the 23rd FG. By the end of October, eight more pilots would join them on the roster of aces.

Chennault has split his forces at the beginning of the summer, placing the 16th and 75th FSs in the west at Yunnanyi and Kunming respectively, and the 74th and 76th FSs on the eastern airbases at Kweilin, Ling Ling and Hengyang. His eastern force, which also included the 11th BS (B-25s), was organised as the Forward Echelon, under the command of Col Clinton D 'Casey' Vincent. Col Bruce Holloway continued as 23rd FG commander.

After three weeks of relative inactivity due to bad weather, the air war over the east China bases re-ignited on the morning of 23 July 1943, when the JAAF sent a mixed formation of bombers and fighters from Hankow to attack Hengyang and Ling Ling. The enemy aircraft took a roundabout route to their targets, and flights from the 76th FS scrambled from both bases to meet them. The Ling Ling-based P-40s made first contact about 50 kilometres south-east of the field. Following their aggressive attack, the Japanese bombers jettisoned their bombs and ran for home,

1Lt Stephen J Bonner Jr scored five victories (and five probables) with the 76th FS between July 1943 and May 1944. All of these kills (and four of the probables) were recorded in P-40s, although he also flew many missions in P-51s following his unit's conversion to the North American fighter in mid-1944. Four of Bonner's victories were scored directly overhead his home airfield of Suichwan, which made them easy to confirm

One of the flight leaders with the 76th FS in late 1943, Capt Lee Manbeck poses in a P-40K at Suichwan. This particular Warhawk (probably 'White 117') was a re-engined aircraft transferred from a combat unit in North Africa, hence the three swastikas painted below the cockpit. Manbeck was shot down in early 1944 after 31 months of overseas service and apparently died in captivity

Fresh from the fight, an excited 1Lt John S Stewart of the 76th FS describes his combat missions of 23 July 1943, in which he shot down two Japanese bombers in the morning and a fighter in the afternoon for his first aerial claims. Behind him is his P-40K, *Lynn II*. Stewart completed a double tour in China, and scored nine victories, before returning home in mid-1944

Texan Capt J M 'Willie' Williams of the 76th FS poses in front of a P-40K. The ace scored six victories in July and August 1943, before being promoted to squadron commander to oversee the unit's transition to the P-51A. He was shot down in a Mustang over Hong Kong on 1 December 1943 and was duly sent home after he returned to base 16 days later. Fellow ace John Stewart succeeded him as CO of the 76th FS

Maj Elmer W Richardson flew P-40K *Evelyn II* with the 75th FS, and it is seen here in late 1943 after its pilot had assumed command of the unit (hence the two white fuselage bands). Note the DF 'football' atop the fuselage immediately behind the cockpit – this aircraft was one of the first P-40s in-theatre so equipped. A second pair of centreline shackles can also be seen beneath the fighter's belly. Finally, kill markings for six of Richardson's eight victories are displayed

leaving their 'Oscar' escorts to tangle with the P-40s. A large flight of 18 Warhawks from the 74th FS also arrived from Kweilin to join the fight.

23rd FG pilots were credited with two bombers and five fighters destroyed in this engagement, with three of the victories falling to 76th FS flight leader Capt Lee Manbeck, and another to future ace 2Lt Stephen Bonner.

By the time the Japanese raiders reached Hengyang, two more flights of P-40s from the 76th FS were waiting for them at 28,000 ft, led by 1Lts J M 'Willie' Williams and John S Stewart. The latter pilot experienced an oxygen system failure whilst he waited for the raiders, so he descended to 20,000 . . . and spotted the incoming enemy bombers! Calling Williams down to take on the 'Oscar' escorts, Stewart ploughed into the bomber formation head-on. His first victim staggered and fell, while gunners from the other bombers fired wildly at the attacking P-40. Stewart shot down a second bomber moments later, and was firing on a third when his own aeroplane was hit hard. He broke off the attack and headed back to Hengyang, where he had to make a belly landing because his undercarriage refused to come down. Later, mechanic's counted 167 bullet holes in Stewart's P-40K, which he had named *Lynn II* after his wife. Williams and 2Lt Dick Templeton were able to confirm two 'Oscars' destroyed in the fight as well.

That afternoon, another wave of enemy aircraft was reported on its way toward Hengyang and Ling Ling, and again the P-40 defenders rose to do battle, led this time by Capt Marvin Lubner. At the same time, Col Casey Vincent led six P-40s up from Kweilin and Col Bruce Holloway flew in to Ling Ling, gassed up, and took off again to join the fight. The P-40s encountered a large formation and claimed six destroyed without loss. Among those credited with kills was Casey Vincent, whose bomber victory took his overall tally to five, thus adding his name to the list of aces.

23 July also saw the arrival of the first P-38 Lightnings in China (see *Osprey Aircraft Aces 14 - P-38 Lightning Aces of the Pacific and CBI* for further details), five twin-engined fighters flying into Kweilin on this day. In keeping with its promise to build up Chennault's tiny Fourteenth Air Force, the USAAF had formed the 449th FS from a pool of P-38 pilots awaiting assignment in North Africa. Once in China, the unit was placed under the temporary command of veteran 75th FS P-40 pilot, Capt Elmer Richardson.

The new P-38 pilots did not have to wait long to see action, for the next morning the Japanese struck at Chennault's eastern bases from Hankow in the north and Canton in the south. The 76th FS added eight victories to its tally at Ling Ling, again without loss, whilst a flight from the 74th that had scrambled from Kweilin added two more kills, but lost a pilot.

Meanwhile, a flight of eight 'Oscars' from Canton managed to approach within 38 miles of Kweilin before they were spotted, and although P-40s and P-38s were hastily scrambled, they were caught from above by the Ki-43s. One Lightning was quickly shot down, but the 23rd FG pilots managed to gain the upper hand and destroy six of the eight attackers – Col Holloway shot down one of the 'Oscars' for his tenth victory. More action followed on 25 July, when 15 Japanese fighters attempted to catch a flight of B-25s landing at Hengyang after a bombing mission to Hankow. Holloway had a patrol of P-40s aloft to protect the recovering bombers, and they knocked down two plus three probables without loss. The B-25s, meanwhile, diverted to Kweilin, returning to Hengyang just before dusk to be ready for the next day's mission.

Five B-25s took off from Hengyang at 0500 hrs on 26 July to attack Hankow airfield once again. Their escorts were P-40s from the 74th and 75th FSs, which had sent seven aeroplanes across from Kunming earlier in the week to bolster the eastern fighter force. Once the 'medium twins' had completed their bombing runs, they were attacked by a large force of Ki-43s, and several bombers sustained damage before the P-40s could intercede. A running fight ensued in which the 75th's Capt Elmer Richardson claimed two destroyed, and another future ace in 1Lt Lynn F Jones of the 74th FS was credited with one confirmed and two probables.

This was the entrance to the cave at Kweilin that housed the operations room for the air-raid warning net. Seen smoking a cigarette to the right of the photograph is 1Lt Lynn F Jones of the 74th FS. His assigned aircraft was P-40K 'White 22', and he scored five confirmed victories between June and December 1943 to become only the second 'home-grown' ace of the 74th FS

Col Vincent sent his bombers and fighters to strike at targets in Hong Kong harbour on 27 and 28 July, and they were barely opposed by the Japanese. The P-40s and P-38s went back to Hong Kong on the 29th, this time to rendezvous with 18 B-24s of the 308th BG flying from Kunming. Again only a few defenders appeared, and the escorts easily held them off. That same day a Japanese force attacked Hengyang, although an aggressive attack led by Capt Bill Grosvenor of the 75th FS threw off the bombers' aim and no damage was done to the airfield.

The morning of 30 July witnessed the last raid by the JAAF in its offensive against Chennault's eastern airfields. The 3rd Air Division sent two formations from Hankow on different routes toward Hengyang in an attempt to confuse the defenders. Unfortunately for the Japanese aircrews, the Chinese warning net was able to plot both tracks accurately, so when they joined up north of Hengyang for their final run into the target, the American pilots were in a perfect position to oppose them.

Led by 1Lt Charlie Gordon of the 75th FS, the P-40s feinted toward a flight of 'Oscar' escorts, then cut sharply into the bomber formation. Four bombers went down, with Gordon, Capt Bill Grosvenor and 1Lt Ed Calvert of the 75th FS, along with 1Lt Vernon Kramer of the 76th FS, being credited with one apiece. Lts Carter 'Porky' Sorenson of the 16th FS, Christopher 'Sully' Barrett of the 75th FS and Tom McMillan of the 76th FS each claimed a Ki-43 destroyed. On the other side of the ledger, two P-40s were shot down and the 75th FS's Lt W S Epperson killed.

It is impossible to determine whether heavy Japanese combat losses or the onset of bad weather caused the three-week lull in air fighting that followed. Gen Chennault made the most of the break by rearranging his fighter forces, consolidating the 449th FS P-38s at Ling Ling and moving the 76th FS to Hengyang, along with two flights from the 16th FS.

The JAAF had a surprise in store for the P-40 pilots as well, for it was beginning to re-equip its fighter squadrons at Hankow with the new Nakajima Ki-44 'Tojo'. This aircraft would give the Japanese pilots a clear performance advantage over their P-40-equipped adversaries.

The 23rd FG's first encounter with the new 'Tojos' came on 20 August 1943, when Col Holloway and Maj Norval Bonawitz, commander of the 74th FS, led 14 P-40s from Kweilin to intercept a raid in bound from Hankow. What they encountered was a fighter sweep by 20 'Tojos' flying at 30,000 ft or higher – above the combat ceiling of the P-40s. The American pilots had no choice but to wait for the 'Tojos' to initiate combat on their own terms. This they did by diving down on straggling P-40s, taking a shot at them, and then zooming back up out of range – precisely the tactics preached by Chennault to his P-40 pilots. Two Warhawks and their pilots were lost, but Capt Art Cruikshank of the 74th was able to claim two 'Tojos' destroyed. The P-40s were in action again that afternoon, knocking down four Ki-43s over Tien Ho airfield at Canton while escorting B-25s. Another Japanese attack on Hengyang the next day netted five more victories for the P-40s of the 76th FS against one loss.

Col Bruce Holloway scored his 11th and 12th kills on these two missions, whilst his 13th, and last victory, came on 24 August during yet a nother bomber escort mission. As he recorded in his diary, Holloway passed up the chance to become the all-time top-scoring American P-40 ace that day;

'We came in with the B-25s and bombed the Wuchang airdrome. The bombing was good. There were several Zeros still over the town, but all were working singly. I made a head-on run with one and shot him down – I could have gotten more but we stuck right with the B-25s and kept the Zeros off them; nobody got hit. We stayed with them for 75 to 100 miles south. At this time we ran across three B-24s up to the left, and they kept yelling about a Zero above them. I saw it and kept watching it – finally it dived down behind the B-24s, pulled up and started west. I turned around with my flight and climbed up fast behind him – a perfect sitter, so I held off and let my wingman (Lt Francis Beck of the 16th FS) get him. We came on home and nothing else happened. All the P-40s got back okay and accounted for ten Zeros confirmed and three probables.'

Two weeks later, Holloway would be promoted to temporary commander of the Forward Echelon while Vincent took leave in the US. This effectively ended his combat flying in China. Holloway would go on to complete a distinguished military career, retiring from the USAF as a four-star general in 1973.

Of the ten kills reported by Holloway on 24 August, two apiece were credited to Capt Art Cruikshank of the 74th FS and 1Lt John Stewart of the 76th FS, making them both aces. One of the original 'school squadron' pilots of 1942, Cruikshank would soon finish his tour and leave for home, although he would return to command the 74th FS in 1944. Stewart flew back-to-back tours without leave, becoming CO of the 76th FS in December 1943 after the unit had mostly converted to P-51A Mustangs.

The 76th FS added two more aces during a morning escort mission to Canton on 26 August when Capt Marvin Lubner claimed one victory for a total of five, and 1Lt 'Willie' Williams got his fifth and sixth victories, plus a probable. Here, Williams describes his last kill, which he achieved whilst chasing off an enemy fighter that was attacking a damaged P-40;

'I turned back, rolled over, and fired way ahead of the Zero. I knew I was out of range but hoped the Zero pilot would see my tracers. He did see them and pulled straight up. Climbing was the thing for a Jap to do, only this time I had altitude on him. When he got to the top of his climb I was almost in formation with him. All I had to do was pull the trigger and let those six 0.50-calibres do the rest. He rolled over with black smoke pouring out of the aeroplane and went into the ground.'

The Forward Echelon continued to pound enemy targets in east China throughout mid-September, its P-40 pilots recording 16 victories up to the 15th of the month. Japanese attacks on airfields in the area had all but ceased by this time, however, although the JAAF did not officially call off its aerial offensive until 8 October. By then it had suffered yet another serious drubbing.

On 20 September the warning net discovered a Japanese formation approaching Kunming from Indo-China, and P-40s of the 16th and 75th FSs scrambled to meet it. This sector of China had been quiet all summer, so the pilots were eager to see some action. Seven P-40s of the 16th FS at Chengkung, led by Maj Bob Liles, made first contact with the raiders, followed by the 75th FS, who hit the bombers hard. Three flights, led by Capts Charlie Gordon, Bill Grosvenor and Roger Pryor, attacked out of the sun and scattered the bombers. Gordon was credited with one bomber destroyed and Pryor with two, both achieving ace status with their fifth victories. Their squadron mates shot down nine more, including two credited to future ace Grosvenor (who would get his fifth on 1 October over Haiphong). The few bombs that hit the airfield at Kunming caused only minor damage, and no casualties. 1Lt Lyndon R 'Deacon' Lewis was shot down, but returned to base unhurt five days later.

ENTER THE 51ST FG AND THE CACW

While the 23rd FG was busy holding the line in east China, big changes were taking shape within the Fourteenth Air Force. The long-awaited build-up, heralded by the arrival of B-24s of the 308th BG and the P-38s of the 449th FS, would pick up steam in September 1943 with the decision to transfer the 51st FG from the Tenth Air Force to China. The move added two full P-40 squadrons – the 25th and 26th – to Chennault's forces.

The 25th FS took over air defence duties at Yunnanyi when the unit moved up from Assam in the autumn of 1943. Here, B Flight poses with *Jeanette*, alias P-40K 'White 208'. Kneeling, from left to right, are William Livergood, Jim Thorn, Joseph Novak and Glade Burton. Standing, again from left to right, are William Southwell, Joe Hearn, David Mumbaugh, Edward Lawler (flight surgeon), Ben Parker, Warren Slaughter and Charles White

As seen in the previous chapter, the 25th and 26th FSs were staffed by a mix of combat veterans who had seen action over Burma, and fresh pilots recently transferred in from the 80th FG. Their equipment consisted of P-40Ks and Ms, with a few new P-40Ns in the 26th.

With the additional units at hand, Chennault reorganised the combat echelons of the Fourteenth Air Force into two composite wings. The 68th CW, headquartered at Kweilin, would cover eastern China with the P-40s of the 23rd FG, the P-38s of the 449th FS and the B-25s of the 11th BS, whilst the 69th CW, headquartered at Kunming, would protect the Hump bases, with the 25th FS at Yunnanyi and the 26th FS at Kunming. B-25s of the 341st BG would also be added to its roster later on. The 16th FS was reassigned to its parent group, the 51st, and the 449th was attached for administrative purposes, although both units remained in east China for the time being.

As this P-40K clearly shows, the 26th FS added distinctive sharkmouths and eyes to its Warhawks several months after arriving in China. The squadron badge in the centre of the mouth shows the 'China's Blitzer' reindeer mascot, complete with P-40 wings, propeller spinner nose and gunsight

While all this was going on in China, another combat wing for the Fourteenth Air Force was being built from scratch at the huge training base at Malir, outside Karachi. This unit would be unlike any other, for the Chinese-American Composite Wing (CACW) was a product of necessity, as much as anything else.

Chinese pilots had been training in the United States since 1941, but the CAF units in China had played very little part in the air war since the Americans arrived. Chennault

knew it would be wasteful for these new Chinese pilots to be assigned to dormant CAF units when he needed combat squadrons to fight the Japanese now. The USAAF at this time was struggling to meet manpower requirements for pilots worldwide, although American industry was pumping out aircraft – in particular P-40s and B-25s – at a breakneck pace. When Chennault proposed to combine the two resources, Chiang Kai-shek and the USAAF readily agreed and the CACW was born.

Chennault had learned from his long experience in China that the CACW needed to be structured in such a way that would not offend the status-conscious Chinese, but at the same time would provide them with effective combat leadership. His first step had been to attract a select cadre of CAF pilots to the squadrons of the 23rd FG in the spring of 1943. Most of these men were subsequently reassigned to the CACW as flight leaders and squadron commanders. They would fill slots in a dual command structure that placed one Chinese and one American officer in each leadership position from flight leader all the way up to wing commander. Newly-trained Chinese pilots would round out the squadrons.

Training of the first three CACW squadrons – two with P-40s and one with B-25s – commenced at Malir in August 1943. When these three were ready to go in October, three more were formed. The first two

Fighter squadrons of the Chinese-American Composite Wing trained at Malir, in India, on war-weary P-40s before moving up to China for combat operations. Here, a Chinese pilot of the 3rd FG gets instruction prior to firing up the engine of 'White 706'. Note how the sharksmouth has been painted out

Chinese soldiers inspect newly-arrived P-40N 'White 655/D2' of the CACW's 32nd FS/3rd FG at Kweilin's Erh Tong airfield. The 28th and 32nd FSs flew their first missions in December 1943, claiming nine victories by the end of the month

Maj William L Turner, CO of the CACW's 32nd FS/3rd FG, prepares for a mission in his P-40N 'White 646' with the help of his crewchief, Sgt Keith Worme. The three victory flags signify kills Turner scored in the Southwest Pacific during 1942 flying P-40Es and P-400s. He would claim an additional five victories in China

On 3 November 1943 1Lt Robert M Cage of the 74th FS shot down a Japanese fighter during an escort mission to Canton. Upon returning to Kweilin he found that the hydraulic system of his P-40N-1 had been shot out during the engagement, so he carried out a successful belly landing. Note the unbordered national insignia and the dark green dapple camouflage on the tail of the now propellerless 'White 41'

CACW P-40 squadrons (the 28th and 32nd FSs) arrived in Kweilin in late November 1943 and commenced operations the following month. By the summer of 1944, the CACW had completed the training of two fighter groups (the 3rd and 5th FGs) with four squadrons of P-40s each, plus the 1st BG with four B-25 units. Although technically part of the CAF, these groups were under the command of Chennault and his Four-teenth Air Force. CACW aircraft were the property of the CAF under lend-lease provisions, and they wore full CAF markings.

The increase in the number of fighters in-theatre also led to a change in the way the Fourteenth Air Force marked its aircraft. By the autumn of 1943, new P-40Ms and Ns were being delivered to China with more

distinctive 'star-and-bar' national insignias, so it no longer made sense to paint out the fuselage stars on the 23rd FG's aircraft. As a result, squadron numbers were moved to the tails of all P-40s, and the following numbering system was introduced: 74th FS, 20-59; 75th FS, 151-199; 76th FS, 100-150; 16th FS, 351-400; 25th FS, 200-250; and 26th FS, 251-299. The 449th's P-38s were numbered 300-350 on their tail-boom radiators. Later, the P-40Ns of the CACW's 3rd FG would be marked with numbers in the 600s and the 5th FG in the 700s. Finally, Fourteenth Air Force bomber squadrons were assigned 50-number blocks.

A DECEMBER TO REMEMBER

On 13 November 1943 units of the Japanese 11th Army moved out of their camps in the Hankow area and headed west toward the Chinese-held city of Changteh, on the far side of Tungting Lake. The primary goal of the manoeuvre was to relieve Chinese farmers in this rice-rich area of their crops, which were needed to feed Japanese soldiers elsewhere. The P-40 squadrons in east China responded ferociously, raining down a torrent of bombs and bullets on the enemy advance, but by 1 December the Japanese had surrounded Changteh and held it under siege. The P-40 pilots then flew their aircraft as makeshift transports, filling belly tanks

Warhawks of the 74th FS await their next mission at Kweilin in December 1943. The pilot of P-40N-5 'White 21' (42-105009) was Capt Harlyn S Vidovich, whose two victory flags appear below the windshield. Vidovich, a full-blooded American Indian (note the Indian head artwork forward of the cockpit), was ferrying a new P-40N from Kunming to Kweilin on 18 January 1944 when he crashed in bad weather and was killed

2Lt Bill Carlton of the 75th FS bemoans the fate of his P-40K *STINKY* after Polish RAF ace Witold Urbanowicz belly-landed the fighter at Hengyang in December 1943. Urbanowicz flew with the 75th on exchange duty for the last three months of 1943, scoring two victories on 11 December over Nanchang. During this time he usually flew P-40M 'White 188' (see *Osprey Aircraft of the Aces 21 - Polish Aces of World War 2* for further details)

Maj Ed Nollmeyer, CO of the 26th FS, talks with his crewchief, Sgt Jerry Dusek, in front of their P-40K ('White 255') at Kunming. The fighter displays five victory flags just below the windscreen, which means that this photograph was taken after 22 December 1943, when Nollmeyer claimed two Ki-43s to take his final tally to exactly five kills. Note that the P-40 still lacks a sharksmouth, despite it having been on strength with the 51st FG for several months. The yellow band around its nose was a squadron marking, as was the badge on the cowling. Nollmeyer was the 26th FS's first ace

with ammunition and food that they then dropped to the Chinese troops defending the city.

The first aerial battle over Changteh took place on 4 December when pilots of the 74th and 75th FSs fought off 'Tojos' attempting to attack the B-25s they were escorting. More clashes occurred as the month progressed, and on 12 December the Japanese struck back with a series of raids on Hengyang. After the first formation of 'Tojos' and 'Oscars' broke off an engagement over the city and headed for their base at Nanchang, Capt Lynn F Jones of the 74th FS gave chase with a fresh flight of P-40s. He caught the enemy formation by surprise near Nanchang and shot down one 'Oscar' for his fifth victory.

On that same day a replacement pilot with the 75th FS recorded one of the more unusual aerial victories of the China air war. Flying in a wingman slot, 2Lt Donald S Lopez lost sight of his flight leader in the haze after their first pass at a formation of Ki-43s. Lopez then saw an 'Oscar' chasing another P-40 and began closing in on it from behind. The Japanese pilot duly spotted Lopez and whipped around in a tight turn to make a head-on pass. Both men opened fire, and Lopez saw his bullets hitting home, but by then the two fighters were practically on top of each other.

The Japanese pilot veered sharply to his right, but the left wings of the opposing fighters struck each other. Lopez felt a jolt and looked back to see the wing of the 'Oscar' separate from the fuselage, sending it whirling down in a crazy dive. The P-40's wing was mangled, but intact, and Lopez managed to land the fighter without incident at Hengyang. Lopez's victory was the first of five (the last of which was claimed in a P-51C) he would score in China. In all, 23rd FG pilots were credited with 16 confirmed victories on 12 December, this haul helping them to set a new monthly group record of 41 kills.

December also saw the CACW pilots of the 3rd FG making their combat debut, and they tallied nine victories during the month. Finally, the 51st FG ended 1943 with a record month for victories thanks to the Japanese twice sending heavily escorted bomber formations up from Burma to raid Kunming, whilst a third raid struck Yunnanyi. The group made effective interceptions on all three occasions, scoring 34 kills in the process. The airbases suffered very little damage from the enemy bombs.

Patched and worn, P-40K 'White 356' of the 16th FS was flown by Capt J Roy Brown in late 1943, probably from Kunming. Either a 'hand-me-down' from another squadron or a rebuilt wreck, this Warhawk carried the name *Ole Hellion* on both sides of its nose. Brown scored four victories, three probables and one damaged with the 16th FS between September 1943 and March 1944

Maj Ed Nollmeyer, CO of the 26th FS, scored three kills during the Kunming raids on 18 and 22 December to become his squadron's first ace. Fellow CO Maj Bob Liles of the 16th FS also 'made ace' during the interceptions of the 18th, claiming a solitary Ki-43 kill (plus two probables and a damaged) to take his final tally to five exactly. At Yunnanyi, the 25th FS made the most of a rare opportunity for aerial combat on 19 December by scoring ten victories. One of its pilots, Capt Paul Royer, emulated Lopez's victory by bringing down a 'Lily' bomber in a collision. Another 25th FS pilot, 1Lt Jim Thorn, was the first to get airborne that day, and he led a flight of four P-40s into the fray. He recalls the scrap;

'I lined up on my target and fired a long burst. The "Lily" started smoking – I briefly fired at one engine and it burst into flames. As I broke away I saw that the other three P-40s had scored telling hits, and the Jap formation was in shambles. By then it was a melee and a wild dogfight, with planes all over the sky. I got a snap burst at an "Oscar" and scored, but then I had fire coming from the rear and broke right, where another "Oscar" shot at me, so I pulled up violently. My plane snapped over, then fell into a spin. I just let it spin to evade. By the time I recovered from the spin, I was way out of the fight, and the Japs were headed back out. I returned to the field and landed. Everyone was surprised to see me, for when I spun out of the fight they all figured I had bought the farm. The alert shack was bedlam – sort of like the locker room of a team that has just won a title.'

As 1943 ended and the new year began, American pilots in China hoped the war would be over by Christmas 1944. The Japanese High Command had different ideas.

The P-40s of A Flight, 25th FS, stand at readiness at Yunnanyi in early 1944. *Mimi* (P-40K-5 42-9870) in the foreground was assigned to the squadron commander, Maj Earl Harrington – note the dual command stripes around the rear of the fuselage. The diagonal line across the right bar of the national insignia was the final remnant of the flight leader's stripe that once adorned this aircraft. Unfortunately, the three-digit tail number of this uniquely-marked fighter remains unknown

THE LONG WITHDRAWAL

The Changteh siege, and the so-called 'Rice Bowl Offensive', petered out in early 1944, but bigger, more ominous clouds were already gathering on the horizon. The war in the Pacific was going badly for the Japanese, and long-ranging sweeps over the South China Sea by Fourteenth Air Force bombers, combined with attacks by American submarines, were seriously disrupting Japanese shipments of oil and ore from South-east Asia to the home islands. At the same time, Chennault's fighter force was continuing to grow with the arrival of two more CACW Warhawk squadrons – the 7th and 8th FSs – in China, whilst on the ground, the best units of the Chinese Army were adding their strength to the Allied ground campaign in northern Burma.

In response to these threats, the Japanese High Command decided that its best course of action would be to mount a massive ground campaign that would conquer all of southern China, and possibly force Chiang Kai-shek out of the war. The offensive, codenamed *Ichi-Go*, was designed both to capture the Fourteenth Air Force's troublesome eastern airfields and to provide the Japanese with a railroad link for hauling war materials all the way from Indo-China through Hankow and on to Peking, Korea, and Manchuria. It nearly succeeded.

On 17 March 1944 Lt Ed Cassada was one of eight 16th FS pilots who scrambled at 1600 hrs following reports of incoming enemy aircraft heading for Chengkung. No Japanese aeroplanes were encountered, and Cassada crashed his then new P-40N-5 'White 356' into a rock pile off to the side of the landing strip during his recovery at the airfield. The unhappy pilot can be seen sitting forlornly on the wing of his *Mary Lee II*

Ichi-Go commenced in April 1944, and gradually worked its way down the Hsiang River valley from Hankow. Chinese forces held the city of Changsha for several weeks, but when it fell Hengyang was left exposed. The Fourteenth Air Force abandoned its airfield in the latter city on 16 June, Ling Ling fell in August and Kweilin in September. From Indo-China, further Japanese ground forces began moving north-east to link up with the advance, targeting new Fourteenth Air Force airfields at Nanning and Liuchow. By the end of the year, the Japanese had completed their rail link, but they fell short of their goal because the railroad was useless as long as it remained vulnerable to air attack. The Fourteenth Air Force, by maintaining air superiority, saw to it that the rail line never went into service. Nor were the Japanese able to use the airfields they had captured.

The P-40 squadrons in China remained heavily engaged throughout the *Ichi-Go* campaign. They had frequent scraps with Japanese aircraft, but their primary assignment was ground attack. Using bombs, rockets and gunfire, they struck at troop concentrations, tanks and artillery at the front, as well as anything moving along the Japanese communication and transport routes. Trucks, trains and river boats were favoured targets, along with bridges and marshalling yards.

The 26th FS had moved a detachment of P-40s to Nanning (a new base about 130 miles south of Kunming) in mid-March 1944. It was from there on 5 April 1944 that 1Lt Lyndon O Marshall enjoyed one of the most spectacular combat successes of the air war in China, destroying four Japanese aircraft in a single mission. He tells the story;

'I was operations officer at Nanning. On this particular day several of our fighters were away from the base on another mission. The five planes

1Lt L O 'Lyn' Marshall became the second, and last, ace of the 26th FS/51st FW on 5 April 1944 when he downed four Japanese fighters near the airfield at Nanning. Marshall's P-40K-5 (42-9734) wore the tail number 256, the name *Jaynie* on its nose and shamrock designs on its hubcaps. Marshall declined to paint victory flags on his aeroplane, however

These four pilots of the 26th FS/51st FG were credited with downing eight Japanese fighters during the Nanning raid of 5 April 1944. They are, from left to right, 2Lt Allen Putnam (two destroyed), 1Lt 'Lyn' Marshall (four destroyed), 2Lt Lloyd Mace (one destroyed) and 1Lt Lex Duncan (one destroyed). A ninth Japanese aircraft was destroyed during this action by 16th FS pilot 2Lt Sam Brown, whose P-40 collided with either a 'Tojo' or an 'Oscar II'. The Warhawk pilot was killed in the collision

and pilots remaining were there to protect the base. The weather was cloudy and rather hazy. We received a warning from the Chinese Warning Net that a force of 32 Japanese fighter aircraft were heading toward the Nanning base. The five of us took off and climbed for altitude. Altitude was important because we could build up a hell of a speed in a dive. The P-40 could out-dive a Jap fighter, but it couldn't turn inside of them.

'We had reached 18,000 ft when we received a radio message that the Japs were approaching the field. There was a solid layer of haze between us and the field, so we couldn't see the Japs. We dove down through the haze and penetrated the Jap formation at about 10,000 ft. From then on it was everyone for himself. Early in the fight I used my speed to great advantage, turning, climbing, diving and of course shooting as soon as I got behind a target. My shooting accuracy must have been pretty good.

'I nearly killed myself during the sortie. In a fight, we operated at full throttle. I had gradually worked down toward the ground, so it was necessary for me to regain some altitude if possible. As I was climbing, my plane flipped over into an inverted spin, which can happen if you reach a

Groundcrewman of the CACW's 32nd FS/3rd FG pose on P-40N *BAD TOM* ('White 648') of Capt Thomas M Maloney at Hanchung during the summer of 1944. Sat on the wing are, from left to right, T/Sgt Jesse Knighton, T/Sgt Keith Worme, M/Sgt John O'Brien, M/Sgt Carleen Robertson and T/Sgt Jim Kidd, whilst S/Sgt Bob Riley is leaning on the fuselage

Maj William N Reed, American CO of the CACW's 7th FS/3rd FG, is flanked by Chinese squadron CO Capt Hsu Chi-Hsiang (left) and vice-CO 1Lt Yang Yun-Kuan during training at Malir in late 1943. Reed, who scored three victories as an AVG flight leader in 1941-42, would go on to become the CACW's top ace with nine confirmed kills. Claiming two aerial victories apiece, Hsu and Yang were awarded American air medals in February 1945

This P-40N of the 3rd FG had its tail thoroughly shredded by a Japanese fragmentation bomb at Ankang in the summer of 1944

1Lt Tom Glasgow flies P-40N 'White 367' *"KLAWIN-KITTEN"* over Kunming Lake during the summer of 1944. This 16th FS Warhawk was usually flown by Capt Carl Hardy, and the single Japanese flag below the cockpit signifies his confirmed destruction of an 'Oscar' on 12 December 1943

stalling point while at full throttle. The P-40 would fall out of the inverted spin much easier if the power was cut – it was almost impossible if the power wasn't reduced. But in the excitement of the fight I failed to cut the throttle. By some miracle, while I was working at the controls the plane came out of the spin. I cleared the tops of some trees by a few feet. Japs were on my tail as I was climbing for altitude. They might have thought they had shot me down when I went into the spin. Anyway, they weren't there when I recovered. My plane did get hit a few times, but luckily I didn't. One of the plane's tyres was shot out, causing me to end up in the ditch alongside the runway when I landed.'

Marshall's four victories (scored against either 'Oscar IIs' or 'Tojos' – the pilot could not be sure of exactly which type of fighters he had engaged so effectively) gave him a total of five kills, and made him the 26th FS's second, and last, ace. The rest of the pilots in his flight

Capt Raymond L Callaway was the top ace of the CACW's 8th FS/3rd FG with six confirmed victories, and he flew this P-40N-20 (CAF serial P-11249/'White 681') in late August 1944. It had been transferred in from the CACW's 5th FG, and carried the name *Shirley II* on the left side of its engine cowling. The 'O3' on the fuselage was an aeroplane-in-squadron marking used sparingly by the 3rd FG. Shortly after this photograph was taken, red 'blood stains' were added to the teeth within the sharksmouth marking. Callaway was made CO of the 32nd FS/3rd FG in the autumn of 1944

A Chinese pilot (possibly 6.5-kill ace 1Lt Wang Kuang-Fu) of the CACW's 7th FS/3rd FG sits on the wing of his rocket-equipped P-40N at Liangshan in the summer of 1944. The Chinese inscription on the upper cowling translates to 'Bullet Proof' or, more generally, 'Invincible'

Members of a USO troupe led by film star Ann Sheridan (second woman from left) had just autographed Lt Col Bill Reed's P-40N 'White 660' *Boss's Hoss* at Liangshan when this photo was taken on 20 August 1944. Ironically, a Chinese pilot 'washed out' the aeroplane in a take-off accident the following day! Reed is partially visible at far left behind the 3rd FG CO, Col Al Bennett. The fighter's four victory flags do not include Reed's AVG kills

accounted for five more victories, but 2Lt Sam Brown was killed when his P-40 collided with an 'Oscar' or a 'Tojo'.

'SLAUGHTERHOUSE ALLEY'

When *Ichi-Go* began, the four squadrons of the CACW's 3rd FG were sent north to oppose a Japanese thrust along the Peking-Hankow railroad line in Honan Province. Operating from bases at Enshih (28th FS)

CACW pilot Maj Thomas A Reynolds Jr did not quite become an ace, although he destroyed more enemy aircraft than any other American fighter pilot during World War 2. Flying first with the 17th FS/5th FG and then as CO of the 7th FS/3rd FG, Reynolds shot down four Japanese aircraft and destroyed an astounding 38 more on the ground for a combined total of 42

When Maj Arthur Cruikshank returned to China in May 1944 and assumed command of the 74th FS/23rd FG, he named his P-40N-5 'White 45' (42-105152) *HELL'S BELLE*. The 74th FS badge appears on both sides of the rudder of this aircraft, and it is fitted with a direction finder (DF) loop on top of the fuselage. Cruikshank was shot down by ground fire in this fighter on 15 June 1944, bailing out over friendly territory and returning to his squadron a few days later. The ace scored his last two victories on 25 June 1944, boosting his final tally to eight confirmed

Hanchung (32nd FS) and Liang-shan (3rd FG headquarters, 7th and 8th FSs), the P-40 pilots kept steady pressure on the enemy troops in an area along the Luchow-Loyang Road that they came to call 'Slaughterhouse Alley'.

It was here on 5 May that the 3rd FG recorded its first aerial victories of the campaign when Maj William L Turner and Capt Keith Lindell of the 32nd FS teamed up to shoot down a single-engined bomber. Moments later, squadronmate Capt Tom Maloney and Lt Col Tom Summers of the 3rd FG headquarters shared in the destruction of a twin-engined transport nearby.

William Turner's share of the victory brought his total to 5.5 kills – he had scored three victories in the Southwest Pacific during 1942, and two more since arriving in China. The 32nd FS commander would eventually run his total to eight victories.

Another combat veteran in the 3rd FG was Maj William N Reed, co-commander of the 7th FS. He had served under Chennault in the AVG, scoring three aerial victories and 7.5 on the ground as a flight leader with the 3rd PS in 1941-42, and he would reopen his account against the Japanese on 16 May with two shared victories and two solo kills, raising his overall tally to six.

As the 3rd FG fought its way through the summer of 1944, aerial victories mounted for its P-40 pilots. One of its emerging aces was Capt Tsang Hsi-Lan, who assumed co-command of the 8th FS in June.

1Lt Henry F Davis Jr was a successful Warhawk pilot with the 118th TRS/23rd FG. Between July and October 1944, Davis (shown here with his P-40N-20) accounted for three confirmed victories and two damaged, all of which were Ki-43 'Oscars'. Two other 118th pilots who scored well during this period were 1Lt Oran Watts (the unit's first ace with five confirmed) and Maj Ira Jones (three confirmed)

Amongst the group of CAF pilots assigned to the 23rd FG in 1943 to gain experience, Tsang had scored his first victory on 31 May 1943 while flying with the 75th FS. He added two more on 2 June 1944, and finished his run by destroying another pair (both 'Tojos') on 23 August while escorting B-25s assigned to bomb a railroad bridge over the Yellow River at Kaifeng. Fellow 8th FS pilot Capt Raymond L Callaway had reached ace status the previous day, downing an 'Oscar' near Kaiyu, on the Yangtze River, for his fifth victory. Two future CAF aces in 1Lts Tan Kun and Wang Kuang Fu of the 7th FS also scored their first victories during the summer of 1944.

The last major engagement of 1944 for the 3rd FG came on 27 October when Lt Col Bill Reed led a mixed formation of 16 P-40s from the group's four squadrons on a 'train-busting' mission. After thoroughly shooting up a locomotive about 20 miles south of Hankow, Reed decided to take a roundabout route home that would lead his formation directly over the Japanese airfield at Kingmen.

The P-40 pilots duly found about nine 'Lily' bombers and ten 'Oscars' circling below them in the landing pattern at the base. Reed was on them

On 30 September 1944, 1Lt John Bolyard of the 74th FS/23rd FG ground-looped his P-40N-20 'White 38' (43-23661) at Kanchow after completing a strafing mission. The Warhawk had been transferred in to the squadron from the 91st FS/81st FG, and retained that unit's diagonal white bands on the rudder, although the fin had been painted out to accommodate the 74th FS aircraft number. The name JOY is barely visible on the P-40's upper cowling. Bolyard went on to score five kills during November and December 1944 flying a P-51C

in a flash, shooting down a 'Lily' in his first pass before running out of ammunition. Within minutes smoking wrecks of Japanese aircraft dotted the landscape around Kingmen.

In all, 16 victories were credited, with the top scorer being Lt Wang Kuang Fu, who shared one 'Oscar' destroyed with 1Lt Heyward Paxton of the 7th FS, and downed two 'Oscars' and a 'Lily' by himself to take his total to 5.5 victories. Future ace Paxton also confirmed two 'Oscars' destroyed. Bill Reed's score now stood at nine confirmed, making him the CACW's top ace. Sadly, he was killed less than two months later whilst

Pilots of the CACW's 26th FS/5th FG pose in front of two 'haze'-marked P-40Ns at Chihkiang in June 1944. Standing, from left to right, are Capt Yao Jei (Chinese CO), Lt Tang C C, Lt Laing T S, Capt Glyn Ramsey, Lt Bill King, Lt Fang Wei, Lt Soo S H, Lt Chang Y K, 1Lt Jim McCutchan and Maj Robert Van Ausdall (American CO). Kneeling, from left to right, are Lt Feng T Y, Lt Wei Shian-Kow (who scored the last P-40 victory of the war), Lt Shu T S, Lt Liu L C, Lt Chang Y S ('Vic'), Lt Yang S H ('Bobby') and future ace 1Lt Phil Colman

Capt Don Quigley of the 75th FS/23rd FG sits on his P-40N 'White 175' RENE the QUEEN at Hengyang in May 1944. This aeroplane was named after Quigley's wife, Irene. Promoted to major and given command of the 75th in June, Quigley went on to score five victories before being shot down north of Hengyang on 10 August 1944. He spent the rest of the war as a PoW

attempting to parachute from his fuel-starved P-40 near Liangshan on the night of 19 December 1944. It is believed that he struck his head on the tailplane of his fighter, knocking him unconscious and preventing the ace from pulling the rip cord of his parachute. Reed fell to his death, 'chute unopened.

– FIRE AND FALL BACK –

For the 23rd FG, the summer and autumn of 1944 heralded a series of leapfrog withdrawals as the *Ichi-Go* advances gobbled up airfield after airfield. Other changes were in the works as well, including the arrival of new P-51 fighters to re-equip the squadrons. This process actually began in October 1943, when the 76th FS received 15 P-51A Mustangs from the 311th FG in Burma. More powerful Merlin-engined P-51Bs began to show up in dribs and drabs during the spring of 1944, and eventually the 76th FS gave up its P-40s altogether. The 74th and 75th FSs would follow suit, but not until the autumn (see *Osprey Aircraft of the Aces 26 - Mustang and Thunderbolt Aces of the Pacific and CBI* for further details).

In June 1944 a fourth squadron joined the group – the 118th Tactical Reconnaissance Squadron (TRS), commanded by the aggressive Maj Edward McComas. The 118th initially flew P-40Ns equipped with aerial cameras as well as guns, although these would give way to 'photo-recce' P-51 and F-6 Mustangs later in the year. The 118th TRS was a pre-war Air National Guard unit from Connecticut staffed by highly trained

1Lt Don Lopez of the 75th FS/23rd FG prepares for a mission in his P-40N 'White 194' *Lope's Hope* at Kweilin in July 1944. Lopez scored four victories in P-40s, then became an ace on 11 November 1944 when he downed an 'Oscar' near Hengyang whilst flying a P-51C

Little Jeep was the P-40N assigned to 1Lt Forrest F 'Pappy' Parham of the 75th FS, and it is seen parked on the line at Chihkiang following the unit's hasty move to this base following the abandonment of Kweilin in September 1944. Its pilot reached ace status in a Mustang when he shot down a Japanese fighter on 11 November 1944 for his fifth victory. Sat behind 'White 165' are Warhawks of the CACW's 27th FS/5th FG, painted in full CAF markings

pilots who wasted no time in making their presence felt. Indeed, by October the unit could boast its first ace, Capt Oran S Watts.

Facing the loss of his Hsiang River valley airfields, Gen Chennault had to find new homes for his Warhawk squadrons. But instead of pulling all of them back toward Kunming and Chungking, he looked east to a Chinese-held pocket of territory between Hankow and Canton. There, he had been stockpiling supplies at the Suichwan and Kanchow bases for months. The 74th FS began using Kanchow intermittently in July, and it moved there permanently in early September, under the command of grey-haired Maj John C 'Pappy' Herbst.

Legend held that Herbst had downed a German aeroplane in the Mediterranean while flying with the RCAF in 1941 (there is not official record of this kill, however), and his performance since arriving in China in June seemed to support it. He scored his fourth and fifth victories (both 'Oscars') on 6 August while leading his unit in a strike against its former base at Hengyang, and with the 74th's conversion to Mustangs in September, Herbst's score really began to rise. By the time he left China in early 1945, his tally of 18 victories tied him with Lt Col Charles Older of 23rd FG headquarters as the top ace in the CBI.

The wear and tear on pilots and aircraft during the summer of 1944 was tremendous, with the following figures for the 75th FS being typical for the P-40 units in-theatre. The squadron had 23 P-40s in combat condi-

1Lts William K Bonneaux (left) and Gene Girton of the CACW's 17th FS/5th FG pose with P-40N *Jo n' DoDo*, which the former pilot flew whilst at Chihkiang. The roommates named the fighter (probably 'White 767') after Bonneaux's girlfriend and Girton's wife. Bonneaux scored four victories, one probable and one damaged between 26 June and 9 November 1944, and Girton was the squadron's engineering officer

Capt Philip E Colman (right) was the 5th FG's sole ace, the 26th FS pilot scoring six confirmed victories between 25 July 1944 and 14 January 1945. Here, he is seen receiving a medal from his group commander, Lt Col 'Big John' Dunning. Remaining in the reserves after VJ-Day, Colman was recalled to duty during the Korean War and duly downed four MiG-15s (and damaged a fifth jet) flying F-86s with the 335th FIS/4th FIW in 1952

tion at the beginning of April, but by 1 June that number was down to 13. It fell by two to 11 on 1 July, before rising slightly in August and September. Likewise, the squadron lost eight pilots between mid-May and 1 October 1944, compared to just two during the same period in 1943. On the plus side, the 75th FS was credited with 35 aerial victories, plus dozens of probables and damaged claims during this period of 1944.

75th FS CO Maj Don Quigley reached ace status on 5 August while flying a weather reconnaissance mission near Hengyang. First, he spotted six 'Oscars' in formation above him at 12,000 ft, and seconds later he saw six more aeroplanes below him. Quigley climbed into the overcast, then dove through the top cover to attack a single-engined bomber in the lower formation. He fired at it from astern, and the aeroplane crashed near the runway at Hengyang while Quigley made good his getaway. His luck ran out just five days later, however, when he was shot down by ground fire and captured. Quigley spent the rest of the war as a PoW.

Future 75th FS ace 1Lt Forrest F 'Pappy' Parham claimed his first victory on 19 August during an early morning sweep of the Changsha area. A former flight instructor, Parham was flying on Capt Joe Brown's wing when they encountered enemy aircraft about 20 miles south-east of Yochow. He followed as Brown dove in behind a single-engined bomber and shot it down with a short burst. Climbing back up, the P-40s were attacked by 'Oscars', and Brown quickly got behind one of them and shot it down too, while Parham climbed on up to 12,000 ft. There, he saw what he identified as a 'Hamp' some 2000 ft below him attacking a P-40. Parham dived down behind the enemy fighter and opened fire. Observing his rounds hitting home, the Warhawk pilot followed the fighter down to 7000 ft, where he saw the pilot bail out. Parham went on to score a further four confirmed victories with the 75th FS, the final two being downed whilst flying a P-51C.

HOLDING OUT AT CHIHKIANG

On 9 June 1944, with the fall of Kweilin all but certain, the CACW's 5th FG moved to the airfield at Chihkiang. The alert shack for two of its squadrons – the 26th and 29th FSs – was located at one end the field, with the equivalent building for the 17th and 27th FS being sited at the other. Like the 16th and 75th FSs before them, 5th FG units painted the front half of the propeller spinners on their P-40Ns white for quick identification in the air. Located some 175 miles north of Kweilin, Chihkiang remained the group's home for the rest of the war, and it was there in April and May 1945 that the Japanese advance was finally halted.

By that time the 5th FG had long since established itself as another top-notch China P-40 outfit. Its reputation for skill and aggressiveness was firmly established in three low-level raids flown against the enemy airfield at Paliuchi, across Tungting Lake, on 14, 24 and 28 July 1944. In the course of the three missions, the group accounted for a total of 64 enemy aircraft destroyed on the ground, 31 probables and 24 damaged, as well as two aerial victories. The cost of this success was just one P-40 shot down and another lost in a flying accident.

The action continued in August, as the group flew 566 sorties in the course of 79 missions, shooting down ten enemy aeroplanes in the process. 5th FG pilots also destroyed 577 sampans, 72 motor launches and 249 trucks.

The group's sole ace was Capt Bill Colman of the 26th FS, who scored his fourth and fifth victories on 21 September 1944 near Sinshih. Flying one of four P-40s providing top cover for six others on a dive-bombing mission, he spotted eight Japanese fighters attempting to attack the lower flight and called in the sighting to his flight leader, Maj Bob Van Ausdall. The P-40s immediately dived into the formation of Japanese fighters, Colman downing an aircraft he later identified as a 'Hamp' (probably a 'Tojo') on his first pass. Descending below the sprawling dogfight before

Mud clogs the flightline at Chihkiang during the winter of 1944-45 as a flight of 27th FS/5th FG Warhawks are 'gassed up' for the next mission. The P-40N in the foreground is *LIL' BUCK*, which was flown by Maj Irving A 'Buck' Erickson. Note the aircraft's chequered propeller spinner and protruding tongue from the sharksmouth. 27th FS CO from January to April 1945, Erickson was credited with 2.5 aerial victories. Something of a ground attack specialist, he also destroyed 21 enemy trucks during the month of February 1945! The 27th FS was the last unit in China to be fully equipped with P-40s, flying them through to June 1945

climbing back up into the fray to damage two 'Oscars', Colman then spotted a third Ki-43 closing in on his tail.

Pushing the nose of his P-40 over once again, he dived out of range of his assailant and then made a violent 180-degree climbing turn to the right, which brought him around on a collision course with the 'Oscar'. The Japanese pilot immediately pulled up to the left, but was attacked by two other Warhawks, so he rolled back into a dive toward Colman. The P-40 pilot half-rolled and put a 45-degree deflection shot into the 'Oscar' from above, which belched black smoke and flames from its wing root. Now in a rolling dive, the stricken fighter flew straight into the ground. Colman got good hits on one more 'Oscar', which he claimed as a probable, before returning safely to Chihkiang.

Among the other pilots confirming victories on the mission were Col Frank Rouse, 5th FG commander, and Van Ausdall, CO of the 26th FS. Colman, who claimed one more kill in China (on 14 January 1945) to take his tally to six, would subsequently add a further four MiG-15s to his score while flying F-86s with the 4th FIW in Korea in 1952.

By the time Phil Colman scored his last China kill, the P-40's days as a frontline fighter were coming to an end. The CACW began converting to P-51s in January 1945, and the Warhawk claimed its last aerial victim the following month. On 8 February Lt Wei Shian-Kow of the CACW's 26th FS spotted a Japanese Ki-57 'Topsy' transport aeroplane near Changsha while on an escort mission. The Chinese pilot swooped down for the kill, but the 'Topsy' spotted him and dove away, spoiling Wei's aim. Aborting his attack, Wei repositioned himself and came in again, and this time he hit the Ki-57 in its wings and fuselage, setting the transport alight. It crashed into the ground, and Wei saw no parachutes before the 'Topsy' hit.

As far as this author can determine, Lt Wei's victory was the last confirmed kill ever credited to a P-40 pilot. The final Warhawk outfit in China – the CACW's 27th FS/5th FG – converted to P-51D Mustangs in June 1945. The Curtiss fighter had served long and well in the CBI, its colourful shark, dragon and skull faces creating a unique place for it in aviation history.

These Chihkiang-based P-40Ns of the 17th and 27th FSs are armed with fragmentation bomb clusters. Photographed in the autumn of 1944, the closest Warhawk is 'Black 765' of the 17th FS. The next three aircraft are recent arrivals in-theatre, hence the chalked sharksmouths in outline only, whilst the sixth P-40 in the line-up has been transferred in from the 80th FG in Assam (it still boasts the group's distinctive 'Flying Skull' marking)

APPENDICES

P-40 Units in the CBI

23rd FG (USAAF)
74th FS – July 1942-October 1944
75th FS – July 1942-November 1944
76th FS – July 1942-May 1944
118th TRS – June 1944-October 1944

51st FG (USAAF)
16th FS – June 1941-November 1944 (attached to 23rd FG 7/42-10/43)
25th FS – June 1941-November 1944
26th FS – June 1941-August 1944

80th FG (USAAF)
88th FS – July 1943-July 1944
89th FS – July 1943-July 1944
90th FS – July 1943-August 1944

3rd FG (CACW - CAF)
7th FS – October 1943-January 1945
8th FS – October 1943-April 1945
28th FS – August 1943-March 1945
32nd FS – August 1943-March 1945

5th FG (CACW - CAF)
17th FS – March 1944-April 1945
26th FS – December 1943-April 1945
27th FS – March 1944-June 1945
29th FS – December 1943-April 1945

Note – The Tenth Air Force's 20th TRS flew P-40s from January to September 1944, scoring one confirmed victory. The CAF's 4th and 11th FGs were also partially equipped with P-40s between 1942-45

Aces who flew P-40s in the CBI

Name	P-40 Victories	Notes
Capt John F Hampshire Jr	13	
Col Bruce K Holloway	13	
Robert H Neale	13	(all 13 kills in AVG)
Col David L Hill	12.75	(includes 9.25 kills in AVG; also 2 kills in P-51s)
Lt Col Charles H Older	10	(all 10 kills in AVG; also 8 kills in P-51)
Col Robert L Scott Jr	10	
Lt Col William N Reed	9	(includes 3 kills in AVG)
Capt John S Stewart	9	
Lt Col Robert T Smith	8.9	(all 8.9 kills in AVG)
Maj Arthur W Cruikshank Jr	8	
Maj Elmer W Richardson	8	
Charles R Bond Jr	7	(all 7 kills in AVG)
Capt James W Little	7	(also had 1 kill in F-82 in Korea)
Maj John D Lombard	7	
Maj William L Turner	7	(includes 2 kills in Fifth Air Force; also 1 kill in P-400)

Name	P-40 Victories	Notes
Col Edward F Rector	6.75	(includes 3.75 kills in AVG; also 1 kill in P-51)
Lt Col John R Alison	6	
Maj Raymond L Callaway	6	
Capt Philip E Colman	6	(also 4 kills in F-86 in Korea)
1Lt Charles A DuBois	6	
Maj Edmund R Goss	6	
Capt Marvin Lubner	6	
Capt Tsang Hsi-Lang (CAF)	6	
C Joseph Rosbert	6	(all 6 kills in AVG)
John R Rossi	6	(all 6 kills in AVG)
Col Clinton D Vincent	6	
Capt James M Williams	6	
Capt Wang Kuang-Fu (CAF)	5.5	(also had 1 kill in P-51)
1Lt Stephen J Bonner Jr	5	
Maj John G Bright	5	(includes 3 kills in AVG; also 1 kill in P-38)
Capt Dallas A Clinger	5	
Capt Mathew M Gordon Jr	5	
Capt William Grosvenor Jr	5	
Capt Lynn F Jones	5	
Maj Robert L Liles	5	
1Lt Lyndon O Marshall	5	
Maj Edward M Nollmeyer	5	
Capt Roger C Pryor	5	
Maj Donald L Quigley	5	
Robert H Smith	5	(all 5 kills in AVG)
Capt Tan Kun (CAF)	5	
Capt Oran S Watts	5	
Maj Albert J Baumler	4.5	(also 4.5 kills in Spanish Civil War)
Lt Col George B McMillan	4.5	(all 4.5 kills in AVG; also 4 kills in P-38)
Maj John C Herbst	4	(also 14 kills in P-51s)
1Lt Donald S Lopez	4	(also 1 kill in P-51)
Capt Forrest F Parham	4	(also 1 kill in P-51)
Capt Heyward A Paxton Jr	3.5	(also 3 kills in P-51s)
Capt Joseph H Griffin	3	(also 4 kills in P-38s, Ninth Air Force)
James H Howard	2.33	(all 2.33 kills in AVG; also 6 kills in P-51s, Ninth Air Force)
1Lt Samuel E Hammer	2	(also 3 kills in P-47)
Maj Witold A Urbanowicz	2	(also 17 kills in Hurricanes with the RAF)
Lt Col Grant Mahony	1	(also 4 kills in Fifth Air Force, plus 1 kill in P-51)
1Lt John W Bolyard	0	(all 5 kills in P-51s)

Note – Those pilots listed without military ranks are civilians who had previously served with the AVG, and who stayed in China for two weeks after the group disbanded to assist the 23rd FG in transition and training. Some sources also list Capt Melvin B Kimball, Capt Wiltz P Segura and Maj Clyde B Slocumb Jr as aces

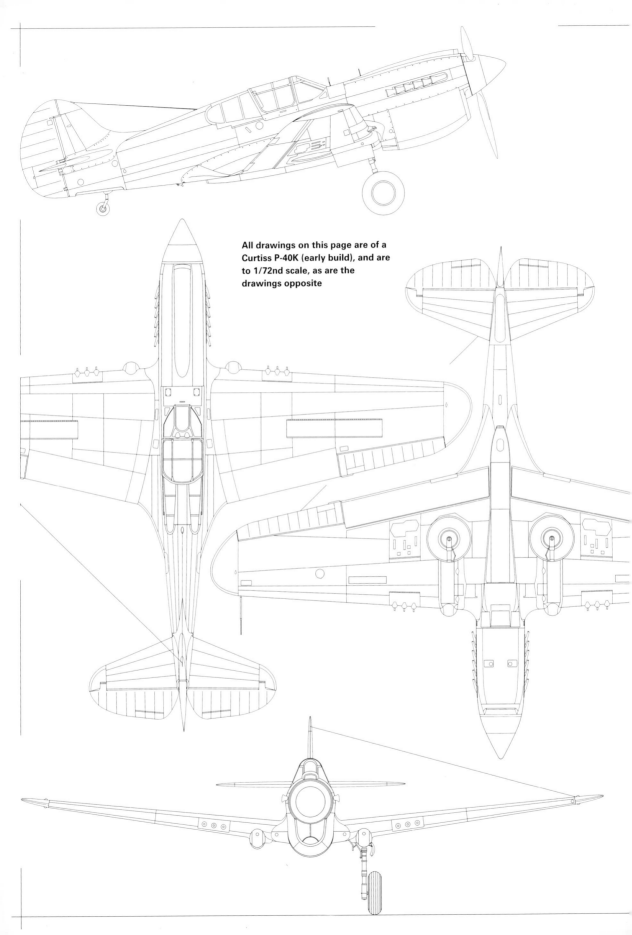

All drawings on this page are of a
Curtiss P-40K (early build), and are
to 1/72nd scale, as are the
drawings opposite

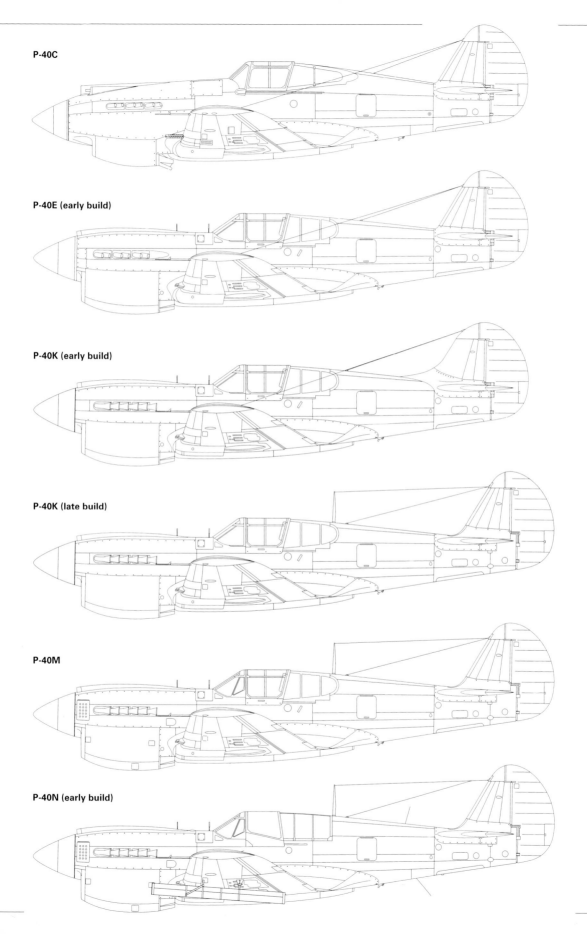

P-40C

P-40E (early build)

P-40K (early build)

P-40K (late build)

P-40M

P-40N (early build)

COLOUR PLATES

1

Hawk 81-A2 CAF serial P-8194/'White 7' of Robert H Neale, 23rd FG HQ, Kweilin, China, July 1942

Neale was the leading ace of the AVG, scoring 13 victories as commander of the 1st PS. He was also one of the pilots who stayed on in China for two weeks after the AVG disbanded on 4 July 1942, helping to hold the line until sufficient USAAF personnel had arrived in-theatre to fill the ranks of the 23rd FG. Neale scored two probables (his final claims of the war) in this aircraft on 4 July over Hengyang. One of the last AVG fighters assembled in Burma in 1941, 'White 7' was painted in the standard AVG camouflage pattern of dark earth and dark green over light grey. The fighter was turned over to the 75th FS when the AVG disbanded, and its Chinese sun insignias were painted out in favour of USAAF stars on the upper left and lower right wings. It did, however, retain both the AVG tiger decal and the 1st PS 'Adams and Eves' badge for an undetermined amount of time with the 23rd FG.

2

P-40E (serial unknown) 'White 104' of Maj Edward F Rector, CO of the 76th FS/23rd FG, Kweilin, China, 4 July 1942

Rector scored a kill in the AVG's first combat, on 20 December 1941, over Kunming. Accepting a USAAF commission to command the 76th FS of the newly-formed 23rd FG following the AVG's disbandment, he scored a confirmed kill and a probable in 'White 104' on 4 July 1942, over Hengyang. One of the first P-40Es delivered to the AVG, this aircraft was camouflaged in dark earth and dark green over medium grey, and carried a Disney-designed flying tiger decal on its fuselage. Fellow aces Bruce Holloway, 'Ajax' Baumler and John Alison also flew 'White 104' at various times before and after Rector returned to the USA in early December 1942. The fighter is illustrated as it appeared in late December 1942 after Holloway had scored his fifth kill in it. Rector returned to China in 1944 to command the 23rd FG.

3

Hawk 81-A2 CAF serial P-8156/'White 46' of 1Lt Thomas R Smith, 74th FS/23rd FG, Kunming, China, September 1942

Smith was one of the original USAAF pilots assigned to the 74th FS, and he scored the squadron's first kill in this ex-AVG aircraft on 8 September 1942. Scrambling from Kunming, he intercepted a twin-engined Japanese reconnaissance aircraft at high altitude and managed to shoot it down – he was awarded a Silver Star for this feat. Smith's only other claim was for a Zero probable during an interception over Hengyang on 10 June 1943. The fighter's red fuselage stripe was a carry-over from its days with the AVG's 3rd PS, and it duly became a 74th FS marking. The 23rd FG continued to fly the old Hawks into the spring of 1943, when the few survivors were retired to the operational training unit in Malir, India.

4

P-40E (serial unknown) 'White 7' of Col Robert L Scott, CO of the 23rd FG, China, September 1942

Scott was a pre-war USAAC pilot who came to the CBI in the spring of 1942 as part of an abortive mission to bomb Japan with B-17s. He was chosen by Brig-Gen Claire Chennault to command the 23rd FG when it was formed in July 1942, and he continued in that capacity until early January 1943. Scott scored his fifth victory in this P-40E on 25 September 1942 during an attack on Gia Lam airfield in Hanoi. He called the fighter 'Old Exterminator', but this name was not physically applied to it. 'White 7' was painted in Olive Drab over Neutral Grey, but the serial number Scott mentions in his wartime autobiography, *God Is My Co-Pilot*, does not match with any known block of P-40E serials.

5

P-40E-1 41-36402/'White 38' of 1Lt Dallas A Clinger, 16th FS/23rd FG, Kweilin, China, Autumn 1942

Wyoming's only ace, Dallas Clinger joined the 16th FS/51st FG fresh out of flight school in the summer of 1941, and arrived in China with the unit when it was temporarily attached to the 23rd FG in July 1942. He recorded his first claims – one Zero destroyed and another damaged – on 31 July 1942, when he and Lt John D Lombard attacked 23 enemy aircraft over Hengyang. This P-40E-1 was almost certainly one of the 68 Warhawks flown off the carrier USS *Ranger* on 10 May 1942 on the first leg of their delivery flight from West Africa to the CBI. It was painted sandy Dark Earth and Dark Green over Sky, and its hubcaps carried a white star on a blue disc – a common marking on 16th FS P-40s. When Clinger was transferred to the 74th FS in early 1943, he flew P-40K 'White 48'. Like this aircraft, it wore the same cartoon on both sides of the rudder, accompanied by the inscription *HOLD'N MY OWN*.

6

P-40K-1 42-46263/'White 24' of 1Lt George R Barnes, 16th FS/23rd FG, Chanyi, China, Spring 1943

Barnes, like Clinger, joined the 16th FS after graduating from Class 41-E in the summer of 1941. His first victory came on 12 November 1942 during a big air battle over Kweilin, and his final two kills were recorded just over two months later at Yunnanyi to bring his score to four confirmed and one probable. The 'Great Wall of the Air' unit badge worn by 'White 24' was inspired by the grateful residents of Ling Ling, who presented the 16th FS with a similarly-marked victory banner following its successful defence of the town in July and August 1942. The fighter was camouflaged in Dark Earth and Dark Green over Neutral Grey, and it also carried the star marking on its hubcaps.

7

P-40K-1 42-45232/'White 161' of Capt John F Hampshire Jr, 75th FS/23rd FG, China, Spring 1943

Hampshire served with the 24th PG in the Canal Zone prior to being posted to China in October 1942. The aggressive pilot wasted no time in getting amongst the enemy, scoring his first two victories on 25 October and three more on 12 November to become the first pilot to reach ace status in the 75th. It is likely that Hampshire scored all of his victories bar the first two in 'White 161', and he was killed in action in this aircraft north of Changsha on 2 May 1943. The fighter was painted Dark Earth and Dark Green over Neutral Grey, and featured the white fuselage band of the 75th FS, in addition to red, white and blue pinwheel designs on its hubcaps. Hampshire was the leading ace in the CBI, with 13 confirmed victories, at the time of his death.

8

P-40K (subtype and serial unknown) 'White 162' of 1Lt Joseph H Griffin, 75th FS/23rd FG, China, Spring 1943

Griffin was one of the first USAAF pilots assigned to the 75th FS in July 1942. He opened his scoring with the destruction of a Japanese bomber over Kweilin on 23 November 1942, and eventually claimed three victories in China with this aeroplane before completing his combat tour. The fighter was camouflaged in standard Dark Earth and Dark Green over Neutral Grey, and featured the white fuselage band of the 75th FS in addition to a red, white and blue pinwheel design on its hubcaps. Like many pilots who flew in China early on in the war, Griffin returned to the frontline to complete a second combat tour, although this time in the ETO. He scored four more kills over Europe during the summer of 1944 whilst serving as commander of the P-38J-equipped 393rd FS/367th FG, within the Ninth Air Force. Like his P-40K, Griffin's Lightning was also nicknamed *HELLZAPOPPIN*.

9

P-40K (subtype and serial unknown) 'White 152' of 1Lt James W Little, 75th FS/23rd FG, China, Spring 1943

Little recorded seven confirmed kills between January and May 1943, and he also had the rare distinction of having scored a confirmed kill in an F-82G Twin Mustang in the opening days of the Korean War. The fuselage number of his P-40K is unconfirmed, but is based on close examination of various photos. The aeroplane was painted Dark Earth and Dark Green over Neutral Grey, and carried the white fuselage band of the 75th FS and US ARMY titling on the undersides of its wings. Later in 1943, either this P-40K or a new one was adorned with both the nickname *POCO LOBO* under its exhausts stubs and the 75th FS 'Flying Sharks' badge on its tailfin. Squadron crewchief Sgt Bill Harris also recalls that he painted a nude 'Petty girl' on one of Little's aeroplanes, although this was later removed. 'The rendition was a knockout', Harris told the author, 'but someone in head-quarters didn't think it was appropriate for a fighter plane'.

10

P-40K-1 42-45911/'White 111' of Maj Grant Mahony, CO of the 76th FS/23rd FG, China, Spring 1943

Mahony was one of the early heroes of the war, having scored four confirmed kills and three probables by February 1942 during the fighting in the Philippines and on Java. He arrived in China in late 1942 and assumed command of the 76th FS in January 1943. Known for his aggressive flying and leadership, he scored his fifth aerial victory and two ground kills on 23 May 1943 at Ichang. The squadron command stripes on Mahony's P-40K were very unusual, wrapping boldly around the fin and rudder – the blue fuselage stripe was the standard 76th FS marking. The flying tiger decal may have been painted over at a later date. Mahony returned to the CBI with the 1st Air Commando Group in 1944, and then went back to the Pacific for a third tour, but was killed during a strafing mission with the 8th FG on 3 January 1945.

11

P-40K (subtype and serial unknown) 'White 115' of 1Lt Marvin Lubner, 76th FS/23rd FG, China, Summer 1943

'Marty' Lubner named this aircraft after his favourite baseball team, the Brooklyn Dodgers. It was camouflaged Olive Drab over Neutral Grey, whilst an earlier P-40K assigned to him (again coded 'White 115') was painted in Dark Green/Dark Brown camouflage with an AVG tiger decal on the fuselage, and lacked the *Dem Bums* titling on the nose. Lubner scored all six of his kills between November 1942 and September 1943, his victims being single-engined fighters. He returned to the 23rd FG for a second tour in the summer of 1945, flying a P-51K named *Barfly* whilst leading the 118th TRS. Lubner is believed to have flown the very last combat mission of World War 2, and he went on to complete a further 21 sorties in F-86s with the 18th FBW during the Korean War.

12

P-40K-5 (serial unknown) 'White 1' of Col Bruce K Holloway, CO of the 23rd FG, China, August 1943

A West-Pointer, Holloway arrived in China in May 1942 with the vague orders to 'observe' the AVG. He soon wangled a combat posting under Gen Chennault, and flew several uneventful missions with the group before it disbanded. Holloway subsequently served in the 23rd FG firstly as its executive officer, then CO of the 76th FS and finally as group commander. His 13th victory, on 24 August 1943, made it a three-way tie with Bob Neale and John Hampshire for the honour of the top-scoring American P-40 pilot of the war. Holloway retired from the USAF as a four-star general in 1973. This Olive Drab over Neutral Grey P-40K-5 may well have carried red/white/blue pinwheels on its hubcaps after its use by Holloway. The fighter was badly shot up on a mission on 8 September 1943 with Lt Fred Meyer of the 74th FS at the controls, and Holloway never flew it again.

13

P-40K-5 (serial unknown) 'White 171' of Maj Elmer F Richardson, CO of the 75th FS/23rd FG, China, October 1943

Richardson, like many of the early aces of the 23rd, flew in the Panama Canal Zone prior to being sent to China in the autumn of 1942. His first score came on 1 April 1943, and by October of that year he was both a six-victory ace and CO of the 75th FS – as denoted by the fuselage bands on his P-40. He claimed his last two kills in December 1943 after being assigned to the 23rd FG HQ, running his score to eight confirmed. Richardson's Olive Drab P-40K shows signs of heavy repainting, which occurred in the autumn of 1943 when the 23rd FG moved its squadron numbers from the fuselage to the tail of its aircraft. The 75th FS painted the forward section of its propeller spinners white at this time as well. This aircraft had previously worn its 'White 171' numbering on the fuselage ahead of a single white stripe, and had its fin adorned with the unit's 'Flying Sharks' emblem. The P-40 also boasted a white ring around the outside of its hubcaps.

14

P-40M (sub-type and serial unknown) 'White 185' of 1Lt Christopher S 'Sully' Barrett, 75th FS/23rd FG, China, Autumn 1943

Barrett flew in Panama and Peru with the 24th FS for a year before joining the 75th FS at Chanyi, in China, in December 1942. On 26 July 1943, he scored his first confirmed victory (plus a probable) during a bomber escort mission to Hankow. Barrett followed this up four days later with his second, and last, kill which he claimed following the interception of 53 Japanese aircraft over Hengyang. The near-daily series of combat missions being flown by the 23rd FG at this time hit the group hard, and in late August Barrett's 'White 185' was one of only ten P-40s within the 75th FS considered fit for duty. This aeroplane was fitted with only four wing guns, which was unusual for a P-40M (it would have left the Curtiss factory with six guns installed). Like all M-models in-theatre, it was painted Olive Drab over Neutral Grey, whilst its national marking consisted of the short-lived red-outlined 'star-and-bars'.

15

P-40K-5 42-9912/'White 400' of Maj Robert L Liles, CO of the 16th FS/51st FG, Chengkung, China, December 1943
One of 68 pilots who flew P-40s off the carrier USS *Ranger* on 10 May 1942, Liles was assigned to the 16th FS in Karachi, and moved to China with the unit in July 1942. He scored one probable over Hengyang during the unit's first engagement, on 30 July 1942, and his first confirmed victory came on 26 December over Yunnanyi. Nearly a year later, on 18 December 1943, Liles claimed his fifth, and last, kill during an interception mission over Kunming. His P-40K-5 (which he named *DUKE*) enjoyed an extraordinarily long combat life, being assigned to the squadron in February 1943, and remaining in service until late July 1944. Again, the aeroplane carried the star marking on its hubcaps, while the rudder motif – a diving eagle holding a 'Tojo' in its talons – was painted on by Liles' crewchief. The ace instituted the unit's white spinner marking during his stint as CO of the 16th FS.

16

P-40K-1 42-46242/'White 356' of Capt J Roy Brown, 16th FS/51st FG, China, Spring 1944
Brown joined the 16th FS as a replacement pilot in June 1943, and scored his first victory on 20 September during an interception over Kunming. He went on to claim three more victories, three probables and one damaged before he completed his tour in June 1944. Although listed as an ace in some publications, Brown firmly maintains that his final score was four confirmed. This aircraft, with its 300-series tail number and white propeller spinner, displays the standard squadron markings adopted in the autumn of 1943, although the victory tally dates it as spring 1944. Heavily weathered in Dark Earth and Dark Green over Neutral Grey, and with a large light-coloured patch on the outer panel of its right wing, 'White 356' may have been transferred in from another unit.

17

P-40N-15 42-106238/'White 367' of 1Lt Carl E Hardy Jr, 16th FS/51st FG, China, Summer 1944
Hardy shot down a Japanese fighter during an interception mission over Hengyang on 12 December 1943, having joined the squadron just days earlier. His only other score was a 'Tojo' damaged during a B-24 escort mission to Yochow on 29 August 1944. On 13 October 1944, whilst serving as D

Flight commander, Hardy was shot up by ground fire in this aircraft during a strafing attack at Kweiping. He nursed *'KLAWIN-KITTEN'* back to his base at Nanning, where he was able to belly-land it without further injury to himself – the P-40 was also duly repaired and returned to service. The unpainted aluminium support strap on the sliding portion of the canopy was a common field modification on Warhawks in China.

18

P-40E-1 41-36391/'White 54' of 1Lt Earl C Bishop Jr, 26th FS/51st FG, Dinjan, India, Autumn 1942
'Duke' Bishop was another of the pilots who flew a P-40 off the USS *Ranger*, being assigned to the 26th FS in Karachi on 26 May 1942 and moving up to Dinjan with the squadron in September to commence combat operations over Assam and Burma. His first encounter with enemy aircraft came on 31 October 1942, when he attempted to intercept a high-flying Japanese reconnaissance aircraft, but had to give up after chasing it for nearly two hours. More than a year later, after the squadron had moved to Kunming, Bishop was involved in two intercept missions that netted him a score of two bombers confirmed destroyed, plus one bomber and one fighter damaged. He damaged this P-40E-1 (a *Ranger* 'original') in a belly landing at Dinjan in early 1943. It was painted in faded Dark Green and Dark Brown over Neutral Grey, with US ARMY titling on the wing undersides.

19

P-40K (sub-type and serial unknown) 'White 82' of Capt Charles H Colwell, 26th FS/51st FG, India, Summer 1943
Yet another USS *Ranger* pilot, 'Hank' Colwell joined an advanced flight of the 26th FS at Dinjan in July 1942, and went on to become one of the unit's most respected leaders. His only claims – one confirmed and one damaged – came on 25 February 1943 during a big Japanese raid on Dinjan. Sadly, shortly after his promotion to the rank of major, Colwell was killed in an accident during an administrative flight on 2 June 1943. 'White 82' carried an unusually large sharksmouth, plus the 'Tom Collins Flight' badge on both sides of its rudder. The fighter's paint scheme was the common Dark Green and sandy Dark Brown over Neutral Grey.

20

P-40K-5 42-9768/'White 255' of Maj Edward M Nollmeyer, CO of the 26th FS/51st FG, Kunming, China, December 1943
'Big Ed' Nollmeyer, who was the first ace of the 26th FS, also joined the squadron from the USS *Ranger* cadre. He recorded the 26th's third confirmed victory on 26 October 1942 in a fight near Digboi, in Assam. A year later, and by then a major and the squadron's CO, Nollmeyer led the 26th to Kunming following its reassignment to the Fourteenth Air Force. The unit adopted the yellow noseband marking when it got to China, whilst the twin yellow fuselage bands on this P-40 denoted its allocation to the squadron commander. Sharksmouth markings were not standardised in the squadron until early 1944 after Nollmeyer had scored his fifth, and final, confirmed kill. A sharksmouth was eventually painted around the squadron badge on 'White 255', but no eye was added. A red and yellow pinwheel design was also painted on the hubcaps. The *Bugs Bunny* badge on the

fuselage was a personal insignia that had also been applied to the rudder of Nollmeyer's previous aircraft, P-40E-1 'White 95'.

21

P-40K-5 42-9734/'White 256' of Capt Lyndon O Marshall, 26th FS/51st FG, Kunming, China, Summer 1944

'Lyn' Marshall joined the 26th at Dinjan as a replacement pilot in February 1943, and he moved to China with the unit later that year. He scored his first victory on 13 March 1944 whilst escorting B-25s to Hainan Island. Marshall's big day came on 5 April 1944, when he led a flight of five P-40s from Nanning to intercept a formation of Japanese fighters attacking the base. Diving through a layer of thin cloud, Marshall and his flight tore into the enemy fighters and destroyed eight for the loss of one P-40 in a mid-air collision. His score for the day was no fewer than four destroyed, two probables and one damaged. Marshall was unusual among CBI aces in that he chose not to display victory flags on his P-40, which was painted Dark Green and sandy Dark Brown over Neutral Grey. The fighter did, however, have shamrocks painted on its hubcaps according to its pilot.

22

P-40K-5 42-9742/'White 209' of 1Lt Charles J White, 25th FS/51st FG, Yunnanyi, China, Summer 1944

White flew his first three missions out of Assam with the 80th FG in August 1943, before transferring to the 25th FS and moving with the squadron to Yunnanyi the following month. He subsequently completed 111 combat sorties over the next 14 months, rising to command B Flight. As luck would have it, the squadron only registered aerial claims on five days during that entire period, and White missed out on all of them. He picked up a shrapnel wound in his left leg during a mission on 3 November 1944, and returned stateside the following month. His P-40K, *Miss Wanna II*, was one of the aircraft that the 25th FS brought with it to China in September 1943. It displays full unit markings, including the distinctive 'Assam Draggins' dragonsmouth on the nose, B Flight badge on both sides of the rudder, and a white propeller spinner with a red tip. The Warhawk was painted Dark Green and sandy Dark Brown over Neutral Grey.

23

P-40M (sub-type and serial unknown) 'White 214' of Capt Paul S Royer, 25th FS/51st FG, Yunnanyi, China, Summer 1944

Royer began flying missions with the 25th FS from Assam in June 1943, and by 1 October he was in China undertaking a B-24 escort mission to Haiphong, during the course of which he claimed one Zero probably destroyed. Royer's most notable sortie occurred on 19 December 1943, when he shot down a 'Lily' bomber and then collided with another one whilst defending Yunnanyi. The collision destroyed not only the bomber but also Royer's P-40, although he was able to bail out of his stricken fighter and return to duty with the 25th FS. The three kill flags on this P-40M reflect his final score of two destroyed and one probable, which made him the unit's top scorer. The angled white fuselage stripe denoted his position as a flight leader. A white ring was also painted around the outside edge of the P-40's hubcaps.

24

P-40N (sub-type and serial unknown) 'White 212' of Lt Fred F Burgett, 25th FS/51st FG, Yunnanyi, China, Summer 1944

Burgett was one of several pilots who trained on P-47s with the 89th FS/80th FG in the USA only to be transferred to the P-40-equipped 25th FS upon their arrival in India. On 24 October 1943, whilst escorting B-24s sent to bomb Hanoi, Burgett experienced engine trouble in his P-40 and carried out a forced landing near Chimming. Assigned a new P-40N ('White 212'), he named it *SING PAO* after the baby daughter of the Chinese doctor who had invited several pilots to his home for dinner. Painted Olive Drab, with a factory-applied dapple of darker green, over Neutral Grey, the aircraft carried the B Flight 'bee' badge on a white disc on both sides of its rudder. Burgett's tour ended when he bailed out of another P-40 and fractured both his legs in the process – he spent the next 13 months in hospitals and rehab centres. To this day, Fred Burgett likes to say that he is credited with destroying two aircraft, 'but unfortunately both of them were our own'.

25

P-40N-1 (serial unknown) 'White 55' of 2Lt Herbert H Doughty, 89th FS/80th FG, Assam, India, Spring 1944

'Hal' Doughty joined A Flight of the 89th FS at Sadiya, in northern Assam, where six P-40s and 12 pilots were stationed to protect the western end of the Hump route. On 27 March 1944 he scrambled with three other P-40s, led by 1Lt Robert D Bell, to intercept Japanese aircraft attacking Allied airfields in the Ledo area. Breaking out of thin cloud at 20,000 ft, the P-40s encountered a mixed formation of 'Helen' bombers and 'Zeke' fighters. In the ensuing melee, doughty shot down two 'Zekes' and a 'Helen', and damaged a second bomber – this proved to be his only encounter with enemy aircraft during the war. All P-40N-1s assigned to the 80th FG, including Doughty's, carried six wing guns. This aircraft also featured a star marking on its hubcaps similar to those of the 16th FS. Finally, the red propeller spinner identified this Warhawk as an 89th FS aircraft.

26

P-40N-1 42-104590/'White 44' of 1Lt Philip S Adair, 89th FS/80th FG, India, Spring 1944

Phil Adair flew 139 combat missions during his 18 months in the CBI with the 89th FS. The first 126 were flown in two P-40s (an N-1 and an N-5) that were both named *Lulu Belle*, whilst the last 13 were completed in P-47Ds. On 13 December 1943, Adair performed a solo attack on a formation of Japanese aircraft attacking Dinjan that subsequently saw him credited with one confirmed destroyed and three damaged. On 17 May 1944 he destroyed two 'Oscars' when his flight was attacked following its bombing run on a bridge near Kamaing, in Burma. Adair brought white tyre paint with him to India, and he used it to paint the whitewall tyres (including the tail wheel) on his first *Lulu Belle*. The hubcaps were decorated with a cartoon of a buzzard carrying a bomb.

27

P-40N-1 42-104??4/'White 71' flown by Flt Off Samuel E Hammer, 90th FS/80th FG, Moran, India, April-July 1944

'Gene' Hammer was the sole 80th FG pilot to score five kills flying single-engined fighters. Joining the 90th FS in Assam in early 1944 as a replacement pilot, he first encountered Japanese aircraft on 27 March 1944 when he was flying as a wingman in a flight of four P-40s protecting Allied airfields in the Ledo area. During a 20-minute battle with the enemy, each of the Warhawk pilots destroyed two enemy aircraft apiece – Hammer's victims were both 'Helen' bombers. Nearly nine months later, and now flying P-47s, Hammer destroyed three 'Tojos' to 'make ace' in the 90th's last aerial engagement of the war. Dubbed *RUTH MARIE*, this well-worn P-40N-1 was Hammer's regularly assigned aircraft in the months leading up to his unit's conversion to Thunderbolts, although he was almost certainly not flying it on the day he scored his first two victories. The fighter exhibited evidence of having previously been numbered 'White 77', and it also boasted two bullet-hole patches on its rudder.

28

P-40N-5 42-105009/'White 21' of Capt Harlyn S Vidovich, 74th FS/23rd FG, Kweilin, China, December 1943

Vidovich was a full-blooded Paiute-Sohone Indian whose grandfather, Wovoka, founded the Ghost Dance religion. He flew his first missions from Kweilin with the 74th FS in May 1943. On 10 June, Vidovitch was preparing to land at Hengyang following a fruitless interception mission when he was told of a second raid approaching the airfield. He climbed out of the landing pattern with his flight and attacked a Zero, which he claimed as a probable. Vidovich went on to score two confirmed victories before he was killed in a bad-weather flying accident on 18 January 1944. His P-40N-5 was fitted with the larger wheels and tyres of earlier model Warhawks, this being a common modification on early P-40Ns in China.

29

P-40N-5 42-105152/'White 45' of Maj Arthur W Cruikshank Jr, CO of the 74th FS/23rd FG, China, June 1944

'Art' Cruikshank was one of the original pilots of the 74th FS, and he was also the first ace to score all of his victories with the squadron. He completed his first tour in October 1943 with six victories, then returned to China the following May to assume command of the 74th. On 15 June 1944, Cruikshank was flying this particular P-40N (which featured the 74th FS badge on both sides of its rudder) when it was hit by ground fire near Chuhow. He bailed out over friendly territory and returned to the squadron just a few days later. Cruikshank scored his last two victories on 25 June 1944, raising his final score to eight confirmed, although he was shot down for a second time the very next day flying P-40N-20 43-22876. Again, he evaded capture by the Japanese, but was sent home when he returned to his unit in August.

30

P-40N (sub-type and serial unknown) 'White 46' of Maj John C Herbst, CO of the 74th FS/23rd FG, Luliang, China, Summer 1944

'Pappy' Herbst arrived in China in the late spring of 1944 following service in Europe with the Royal Canadian Air Force. He flew his first missions with the 76th FS, then assumed command of the 74th FS on 30 June 1944 after Maj Cruikshank was shot down. Although Herbst is best known for being a top Mustang ace, he also flew this particular

P-40N during the summer of 1944. On 8 August he was leading three flights of Warhawks when they encountered a large enemy formation over Hengyang – Herbst downed two Ki-43s to 'make ace'. He finished the war with 18 victories, but was killed on 4 July 1946 flying a P-80 jet during an Independence Day airshow in San Diego, California. All of Herbst's fighters were named in honour of his son, Tommy.

31

P-40N-20 43-23661/'White 38' of 1Lt John W Bolyard, 74th FS/23rd FG, Kanchow, China, Summer/Autumn 1944

Bolyard flew P-40s with the 74th FS for the first ten months of 1944, during which time he scored just one ground kill. His P-40N had been transferred in from the 91st FS/81st FG at Chengtu, and retained that unit's diagonal white bands on its rudder, although the fin was painted out to accommodate the 74th FS aircraft number. On 30 September 1944 Bolyard ground-looped this P-40 at Kanchow after flying a strafing mission against Nanchang airfield. He went on to score five kills in a P-51C during November and December 1944.

32

P-40N-20 43-23400/'White 175' of Maj Donald L Quigley, CO of the 75th FS/23rd FG, Kweilin, China, August 1944

Don Quigley flew 24 missions with the 90th FS/80th FG in Assam before transferring to China in January 1944. He assumed command of the 75th FS in June 1944, and his first victory came on 5 July when he destroyed an 'Oscar' (he also claimed one probable and two damaged) whilst escorting B-25s sent to bomb Tungcheng. Quigley scored his fourth and fifth kills on 4 and 5 August 1944, but he was then shot down by ground fire when flying this aeroplane – named for his wife Irene – north of Hengyang five days later. Quigley bailed out and was quickly captured by Japanese soldiers. He spent the next 13 months in PoW camps in Hankow, Shanghai and Sapporo, on the Japanese island of Hokkaido.

33

P-40N-20 43-23266/'White 194' of 1Lt Donald S Lopez, 75th FS/23rd FG, Kweilin, China, July 1944

Don Lopez joined the 75th FS as a replacement pilot in November 1943. On 12 December 1943, he destroyed an 'Oscar' by colliding with it near Hengyang, the impact tearing the wingtip off his P-40K. Lopez had scored five kills and five damaged (all Ki-43s) by November 1944. In mid-June 1944, this aircraft was struck in the nose by the wingtip of a P-51 in a taxying accident at Kweilin. The name *LOPE'S HOPE* was added to the P-40's upper cowling following the accident.

34

P-40N (sub-type and serial unknown) 'White 165' of 1Lt Forrest F Parham, 75th FS/23rd FG, Kanchow, China, Autumn 1944

A former enlisted man, 'Pappy' Parham was older than most replacement pilots were when he joined the 75th FS at Kweilin in July 1944. His unit was heavily engaged opposing the Japanese advance down the Hsiang River valley at that time, and Parham destroyed his first enemy aeroplane (an 'Oscar', over Yochow on 19 August. Parham withdrew with the unit to Chihkiang the next month, where he ran his score up to five destroyed, two probables and five damaged. Note the extra support strap added to the sliding portion of his P-40's canopy. Parham named all his fighters *Little Jeep*.

35

P-40N-5 42-105427 (CAF serial P-11139)/'White 646' of Maj William L Turner, CO of the CACW's 32nd FS/3rd FG, Kweilin, China, Spring 1944

Bill Turner scored his first three victories during the fighting over Java and New Guinea in 1942, then returned to action in December 1943, when he led the Chinese-American 32nd FS into combat from Kweilin. His combat experience quickly showed, for he destroyed a 'Tojo' on 23 December over Canton. He rounded out his scoring at eight victories with a 'Tojo' destroyed on 25 August 1944. Turner continued to fly in the frontline until 19 December 1944, when he broke his leg during a night parachute jump. The P-40N-5 shown here was destroyed on the ground at Hanchung on 6 June 1944. Like all CACW aircraft, it was the property of the Chinese Air Force, hence the CAF markings. National markings were not applied to the wing uppersurfaces on CACW P-40s.

36

P-40N-20 CAF serial P-11461/'White 660' of Lt Col William N Reed, CO of the CACW's 7th FS/3rd FG, Liangshan, China, August 1944

Bill Reed fought a long war, scoring his first victory on 20 December 1941 over Rangoon with the AVG. His final tally with the group was three aerial victories and seven destroyed on the ground. He returned to China in the spring of 1944 as the co-commander of the 7th FS, and he duly claimed six confirmed victories and three probables with the unit – his last success came on 27 October 1944 at Kingmen. Reed was killed parachuting from his P-40 on the same night that Turner broke his leg. *BOSS'S HOSS* was autographed on its cowling by film star Ann Sheridan, and members of her USO troupe, at Liangshan on 20 August 1944. Crewchief Homer Nunley had the nickname *Jug's Plug* painted on the right side of the fighter's nose. The upturned sharksmouth was a distinctive marking of the 7th FS, but the white propeller spinner was exclusively worn by Reed's P-40.

37

P-40N-5 CAF serial P-11151/'White 663' of Capt Wang Kuang Fu, CACW's 7th FS/3rd FG, Laohokow, China, January 1945

A flight leader with the 7th FS, Wang had earned his wings in 1939 at Claire Chennault's CAF flying school. He scored his first victory on 25 June 1944, and went on to become the leading CAF scorer within the CACW with 6.5 kills in the air. His aircraft's nickname 'Great Grandfather – Commander' (in Chinese characters) referred to a heroic prime minister of the Chow Dynasty. The fighter was damaged in a landing accident at Liangshan on 7 May 1944, repaired, and then wrecked again in January 1945 at Laohokow. The 'White 13' on the rear fuselage was an aeroplane-in-squadron marking from a system used intermittently within the 3rd FG.

38

P-40N-15 CAF serial P-11249/'White 681' of Capt Raymond L Callaway, CACW's 8th FS/3rd FG, Liangshan, China, August 1944

Ray Callaway was a P-47 instructor in the US prior to obtaining a combat posting to the CBI in 1943. He helped train the 8th FS at Malir, then moved with the squadron to China in early 1944. On 9 June 1944, Callaway destroyed one Oscar and probably destroyed a second one at Ichang for his first claims. He shared in the destruction of a Ki-43 with Capt Coyd Yost on 17 September 1944 near Yiyang, which raised his final score to six destroyed, one probable and two damaged. *SHIRLEY II* was transferred to Callaway's unit from the CACW's 5th FG in the early summer of 1944. The 'White 03' on the fuselage identifies it as an 8th FS aircraft. Whilst with the 5th FG, it had carried a 'Black 745' on the rudder, along with the unit's distinctive haze grey rudder marking.

39

P-40N (sub-type and serial unknown) 'Black 726' of Col John A Dunning, CACW's 5th FG HQ, Chihkiang, China, Summer/Autumn 1944

A former gunnery instructor, 'Big John' Dunning was serving as the deputy commander of the 5th FG when he led the group's first two squadrons over the Hump to China in March 1944. He scored two aerial victories during August and assumed command of the 5th in November. One of the original P-40Ns allotted to the group, 'Black 726' was named after Dunning's wife. It bore a distinctive 'haze' paint scheme designed to break up the familiar outline of the P-40 when seen in the sky. Pale 'haze' grey was applied to the front of the spinner, leading edges of the wings, wing tips, horizontal stabilator tips and in a wedge on both sides of the rudder. The scheme worked too well, for several aircraft were attacked by friendly P-40s in their first few weeks in China! The haze scheme was soon overpainted on all P-40s except this one.

40

P-40N (sub-type and serial unknown) 'Black 767' of Capt William K Bonneaux, CACW's 17th FS/5th FG, Chihkiang, China, Summer/Autumn 1944

Bonneaux scored four confirmed victories, one probable and one damaged between June and November 1944 whilst serving as a flight commander with the 17th FS. The tail number of his P-40 remains unconfirmed, but it is based on the fact that Bonneaux later flew a similarly-marked P-51 when he commanded the 17th. This aeroplane, along with Bonneaux's Mustang, were named *JO 'n DO DO* by the pilot and his roommate, Lt Gene Girton, who was the unit's engineering officer. Bonneaux's girlfriend at the time was named Josephine, and Girton's wife was Doris. Girton explained this unique nickname to the author in 1983; 'One night over our daily allowance of Jing Bao juice, "Bonnie" and I decided we should name the plane after his girlfriend and my wife so that it would be assured of tender loving care. So it was that *JO 'n DO DO* was born'. The P-40 was eventually destroyed in a landing accident whilst being flown by another pilot.

Back cover photograph

A mixed line-up of P-40Ks and Ms from the 16th FS/51st FG are prepared for their next mission at Chengkung in late 1943. The K-model in the foreground carries the nickname *Lady Eleanor* above its sharksmouth

INDEX

Figures in **bold** refer to illustrations